THE Baseball SONGBOOK

From The
Baseball Library
Of
Joseph Giannatelli

SONGS AND ... OF AME... ...ARLY YEARS ...STIME

Alfred Publishing Co., Inc.
16320 Roscoe Blvd., Suite 100
P.O. Box 10003
Van Nuys, CA 91410-0003
alfred.com

ISBN-10: 0-7390-4690-X
ISBN-13: 978-0-7390-4690-6

TABLE OF CONTENTS

INTRODUCTION

Baseball, baseball, ain't it a wonderful game...
*   -"Gee! It's A Wonderful Game," 1911*

Almost 50 years before Ring Lardner penned these lyrics, baseball was being celebrated in song as our "national game" in the 1869 composition "Hurrah for Our National Game" ("...Then hurrah for our national game, Hurrah here's a cheer for its well-earned fame..."). As early as 1867, "Base Ball Fever" summed up the nation's attitude toward the game ("...For ev'ry baby young and old has got the base ball fever...").

There are a few earlier compositions inspired by baseball, such as "The Baseball Polka" (1858) and "The Home Run Quick Step" (1861), but since they are strictly instrumental pieces, they are not included in this collection.

Neither of our other two long-time popular team sports, football and basketball, has generated a repertoire of song that comes anywhere close to the number of songs that were inspired by baseball. (Yes, there are college football fight songs, but those are restricted in interest and performance—when they are sung at all—to the individual campuses or alumni get-togethers.*) And when was the last time you heard a basketball team song or, for that matter, a song about basketball?

There are literally hundreds of baseball-inspired songs to choose from, dating back from the mid-19th century to well into the 20th. They are descriptive, humorous, corny and inspirational. They root for teams ("Our Noble Giant Nine," 1889) and against the umpire ("The Umpire Is a Most Unhappy Man," 1905). They glorify the players ("Stars of the National Game," 1908) and revile the bums ("Jake! Jake! The Yiddisher Ball-Player," Irving Berlin's 1913 contribution to the repertoire). They deal with events on the field ("Slide, Kelly, Slide," 1899) and in the stands ("I've Been Making a Grandstand Play for You," 1911). Their musical styles represent the periods in which they were composed: marches, ragtime, waltzes, two-steps, polkas, jazz, etc. Their poetic language also mirrors the imagery of their time: from the mid-19th century flowery and high-falutin'

For peer and peasant, man and boy,
There's none the game can yield.
Both rich and poor delight to show
Their prowess in the field...
*   -"The Base-Ball," 1874*

to the raucous and jazzy lingo of the first decades of the 20th century.

That's the baseball glide,
It's a riot,
I can't keep quiet,
I want to try it...
*   -"The Baseball Glide," 1911*

One of the most interesting songs, from a historical perspective, is "The Fed's [sic] Are Here to Stay" (1914), which extols the glory of the ill-fated Federal League, the so-called "Third Major League," which managed to survive just two seasons—1914 and 1915. A brief history of the Federal League is found appended to the song "The Feds Are Here to Stay." (I've taken the liberty of dropping the ill-placed apostrophe from the original title.)

It is also interesting to note in passing how the very name of the game fluctuated, as reflected in some song titles, from "base ball" ("Base Ball Fever," 1867) to "base-ball" ("The Base-Ball," 1874) before finally settling on "baseball."

The choice of material in this book is based on textual interest and inherent musical value (i.e., "singability"). They are presented not so much as museum pieces but as songs that people did sing and would actually sing today if given the opportunity. Among the composers and lyricists found are such luminaries as Ring Lardner ("Gee! It's a Wonderful Game," 1911), George M. Cohan ("Take Your Girl to the Ball Game," 1908) and Irving Berlin (the aforementioned "Jake! Jake!").

Speaking of "Jake," we must mention the popularity of so-called ethnic humor and the use of dialects and "accents" in the lyrics of songs in the late-19th and early-20th centuries. Popular comic stock characters on the vaudeville and music hall stages, drawn from the arriving immigrants that flocked to our shores in those days, were often presented in an "amusing," sentimental, but sometimes less than flattering light ("Macaroni Joe" [1910], "Chinatown, My Chinatown" [1910], "Hello Wisconsin, Won't You Find My Yonnie Yonson" [1917], and many others of the same genre). In the realm of the baseball song, we find numerous "Irish" songs—due in great measure to the relatively large number of players with identifiable Irish surnames. These generally present the imaginary hero as an unfortunate cross between a buffoon and a drunkard. Among them are "Finnegan, the Umpire"

---

* With the possible exception of Tom Lehrer's "Fight Fiercely, Harvard."

(1890), "O'Grady at the Game" (1891), and "McGuffin's Home Run" (1891), whose subtitle "Comic Song and Chorus" prepares the listener for what is to come.

The venerable minstrel show presented the "Negro" frozen in some antebellum never-never land, happily singing and dancing his cares away. These so-called "coon songs," which purported to describe black American life ("Under the Bamboo Tree" [1902], "At a Georgia Camp Meeting" [1897], "Rufus Rastus Johnson Brown, What You Gonna Do When the Rent Comes 'Round?" [1905]), were more often than not composed by white songwriters—such as "Brother Noah Gave Out Checks for Rain" (1906), which is found in this collection.

These pseudo-ethnic numbers should be understood as products of another era that we now consider to be stereotypes but were accepted as the norm then. This not to say all such material is inherently offensive. We must approach each song in the spirit of its time.

Surprisingly, what was not found were songs growing out of the Negro Leagues. One would have thought that in view of the wealth of songs covering the African-American experience this would have been a rich source of contemporary material. When I contacted Raymond Doswell, the curator of the Negro Leagues Baseball Museum in Kansas City, Missouri, I was told that, to the best of their knowledge, no such songs exist. At least, they have not been published.

Another aspect of the changing styles of the songs is found in the cover art of the sheet music. Great care was taken to make each piece of sheet music as visually attractive as possible. They had to catch the eye as well as the ear. They had to look good on the piano rack—for in the years before recordings and radio brought music into the home, the piano was the essential source of domestic music making. And even after phonograph recordings and radio broadcasts

took over the dissemination of songs (pushing the venerable piano off center stage), great care was still lavished on elaborate, full-color cover illustrations.

Speaking of pushing the piano off center stage, the composers whose works are included here never dreamed that the guitar would come to be, at the very least, an equal partner to the piano in America's "parlors," as they used to call them. Guitar players using this collection will be delighted to find the songs presented in guitar-friendly keys.

So here they are, a bunch of baseball ballads compiled for your singing pleasure, just waiting to be brought to life again. And for those of you who can't read music well enough to get the hang of them, a CD is included with a partial sample of each song to get you started.

I would like to thank Margaret N. Burri (Curator of Manuscripts at the Milton S. Eisenhower Library, Special Collections, Johns Hopkins University) and her staff for their invaluable help in providing legible copies of many of the songs and all of the original sheet music covers used in this book.

I was fortunate to have an editor, Link Harnsberger, who as a dyed-in-the-wool baseball fan, went far beyond the call of duty to come up with all the rare photos in this book. These candid photos, along with the historic, original sheet music covers, give this book that wonderful old-time baseball flavor.

Play ball!

Jerry Silverman

ABOUT THE AUTHOR

The many facets of Jerry Silverman's musical background and experience (including a master's degree in musicology from New York University) combine to make him one of America's outstanding folksingers, guitar teachers and most prolific authors of music publications. He has published over 200 books, which have sold in the millions, including folksong collections, anthologies and method books for guitar, banjo and fiddle. Among these books are "The Undying Flame: Ballads and Songs of the Holocaust," "Of Thee I Sing—Best Loved American Patriotic Songs," "The Immigrant Songbook" and "The Guitarist's Guide and Almanac." He has taught hundreds and hundreds of people, young and old, the joys of making music on the guitar and has performed widely in concerts in the U.S. and abroad. To learn more about Jerry and his publications, you can visit his website: www.jerrysilverman.org

Photo: David Ranz

THE BAT AND THE BALL
1867

Echoes of the Civil War are readily apparent in this song, which was composed just two short years after that conflict ended. The opening line, "We come from the mountains," was evidently "borrowed" from "The Old Granite State," a song written by Jesse Hutchinson some years earlier. The Singing Hutchinson Family wrote and performed Abolitionist songs in the 1840s, 1850s and into the Civil War. Hailing from New Hampshire, the group's signature number was "The Old Granite State," which they used to open every concert.

We have come from the mountains,
We have come from the mountains,
We have come from the mountains
Of the Old Granite State...

Another song, which would have been familiar to everyone at the time, was "The Battle Cry of Freedom" (1862) by George F. Root. The song was sung throughout the war by Union and Confederate soldiers (who had their own version). By 1867, it had sold over 350,000 copies in its original version. M. C. Johnson, who wrote the lyrics for "The Bat and the Ball" that year, unquestionably knew the refrain,

The Union forever,
Hurrah, boys, hurrah...

when he penned

Then hurrah, boys, hurrah,
For the Ball and the Bat...

In addition to these references to well-known Civil War songs, the whole tone of "The Bat and the Ball," with its martial air and thinly veiled references to the war, could not have escaped notice:

We gather in numbers on our field once again...
The contest is bloodless...
And victors and vanquished are friends as before...

Since the actual terminology of the game was relatively new to many, Johnson felt constrained to enclose in quotation marks such words and phrases as "field," "muffing," "home runs," "catches on the fly," "hot one," "tally," "sent us to the field" and even "Base Ball" itself.

Civil War soldiers from Fort Sumter in 1861. Captain Abner Doubleday, considered the inventor of baseball, is at the lower left.

THE BAT AND THE BALL

Words by
M. C. Johnson

Music by
Max

1. We__ come from the moun - tains, we come from the plains, We gath - er in num - bers on our field once a - gain; So__ stand to your bas - es, and "field" it with care, No__ "muf - fing" of balls as they fly thro' the air.

Chorus

Then hur - rah boys, hur - rah for the Ball and the Bat, That serves us for ac - tion, with mus - cles com - pact. 'Tis the pride of our na - tion, the glo - ry of all, Then hur - rah boys, hur - rah, for the Bat and the Ball.

We gather by nines for our national game,
The contest is bloodless, and victory the same;
And victors and vanquished are friends as before.
Then firm on your "bases," but rally to score.
Chorus

Hurrah for the "home runs" – "fouls" are barred, you know,
While "catches on the fly" are just the thing, ho, ho!
Now give them a "hot one," a "tally" it may yield.
But no! they've held the ball, and "sent us to the field."
Chorus

Now "nine" call the scorers – "innings" lost and won,
And in the height of mirth we end our matchless fun.
Our frames have grown stronger and health's ruddy glow.
We've won by our practise of "Base Ball" – ha! ho, ho!
Chorus

Tobacco label, ca. 1869.

Union prisoners, ca. 1863.

THE BASE BALL FEVER
1867

Lew Simmons, Esq., (1838–1911) to whom H. Angelo dedicated "(The) Baseball Fever," was a "tambo"—a comic blackface performer in Simmons and Slocum's Minstrels. He also owned a financially shaky sandlot baseball team in Philadelphia, which he sold to

Cornelius McGillicuddy, better known as Connie Mack, just in time for that team to join the new American League as the Philadelphia Athletics in 1901. Mack's association with the Athletics earned him millions and lasted 50 years until his retirement in 1951.

Connie Mack, ca. 1887.

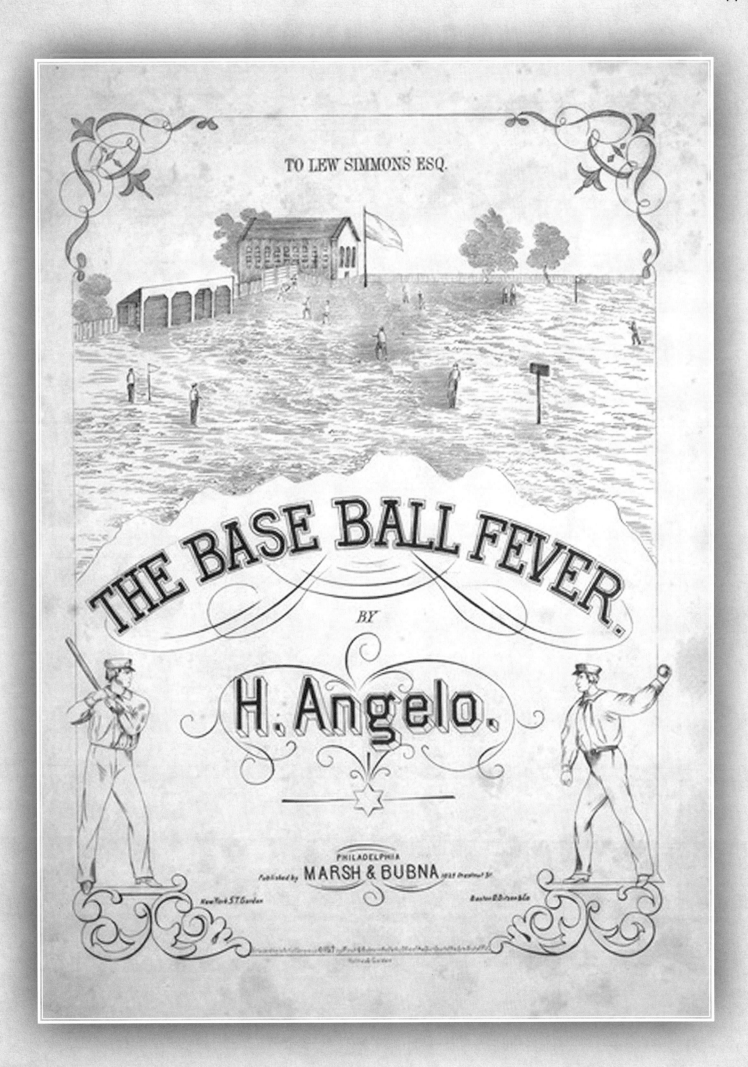

THE BASE BALL FEVER

Words and Music by
H. Angelo

Allegretto*

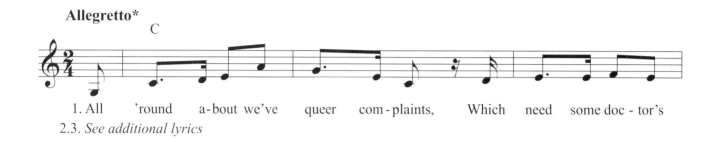

1. All 'round a-bout we've queer com-plaints, Which need some doc-tor's
2.3. *See additional lyrics*

patch - ing; But some - thing there is on the brain, Which

seems to me more catch - ing. 'Tis__ rag - ing too, both

far and near, Or else I'm a de - ceiv - er. I'll

tell you what it is, now, plain: It is the Base Ball fe - ver.

*Tempo indications are given only when they appear in the original sheet music.

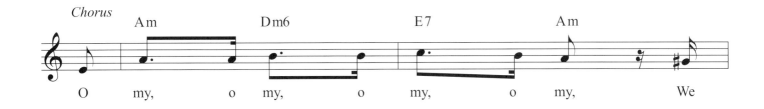

Chorus

O my, o my, o my, o my, We

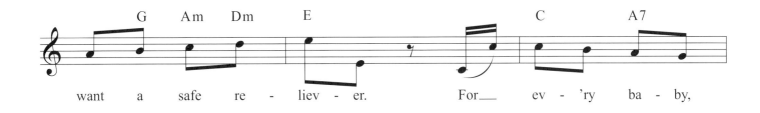

want a safe re - liev - er. For__ ev - 'ry ba - by,

young and old Has got the Base Ball fe - ver.

ADDITIONAL LYRICS

Our merchants have to close their stores,
Their clerks away are staying.
Contractors, too, can do no work,
Their hands are all out playing.
There's scarce a day that folks don't run,
As true as I'm a 'li[e]ver,
To see a match 'bout to be played,
'Cause they have caught the fever.
Chorus

Our little boys as well as big,
All to the Bat are taking;
And smarter folks are coining cash,
At Bat and Base Ball making.
You cannot walk along he street,
I'll bet my patent lever,[1]
That two boys ain't a-playing catch,
'Cause they've got the Base Ball fever.
Chorus

To be in fashion, ladies, too,
In place of Waterfalls,[2] sirs,
Way back behind the ears they wear
An awful big Base Ball, sirs.
I shouldn't wonder but 'ere long,
Each Miss, if you'll perceive her.
Will carry Bats all through their hair –
'Cause she too has the fever.
Chorus

Our papers teem with Base Ball news,
Four columns good and over.
Our stores now sell more Bats and Balls
Than would three acres cover.
We've clubs no end, and players sharp,
But I will bet my Beaver,[3]
That I can catch as well as they,
For I have kotcht the fever.
Chorus

1. leather (?)
2. style of wearing hair in long wave-like folds
3. beaver hat

CATCH IT ON THE FLY
1867

It is interesting to note the use of quotation marks to set off the still developing vocabulary of baseball: "Fly," "Home Base," "tally" and "Regulation" (which referred to the newly standardized playing field dimensions). In the era of traveling medicine shows and patent medicines guaranteed to cure every malady known to man and woman, here we have the promise that baseball will "make the weak man strong" and "brighten every eye."

The lyricist, whose name is indicated on the sheet music only as "Bisco," may very well be John Bisco, the former publisher of the literary magazine *Broadway Journal* (who briefly employed Edgar Allen Poe in 1845 as an editor, before selling it to him for 50 dollars.)

In the presidential election campaign of 1864, in support of Lincoln and Johnson, L. B. Starkweather composed the music for "Liberty's Call, or Hurrah for Abe and Andy."

Freemen rouse in strength divine
And shout for Abe and Andy,
Bright the stars of freedom shine,
Hurrah for Abe and Andy!

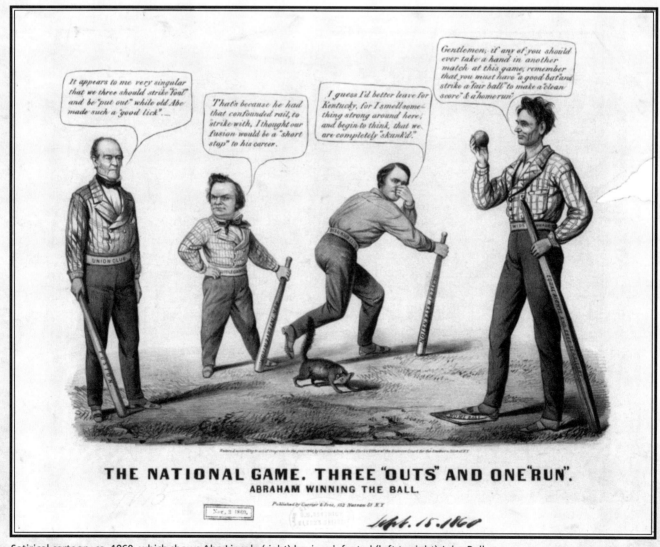

Satirical cartoon, ca. 1860, which shows Abe Lincoln (right) having defeated (left to right) John Bell, Stephen A. Douglas and John C. Breckinridge.

CATCH IT ON THE FLY

Words by
Bisco

Music by
L. B. Starkweather

1.Come jol-ly com-rade, here's the game That's play'd in o-pen air, Where clerks and all the in-door men Can prof-it By a share; 'Twill make the weak man strong a-gain, 'Twill bright-en ev-'ry eye, And all who need such ex-er-cise Should catch it on the "Fly."

Chorus

Play a-way, play a-way, Catch it on the "Fly." When you go to bat, boys, Send it thro' the sky, For

old "Reg - u - la - tion," Where - ev - er you may go,

Bright - ens up the coun - ten - ance, And makes a health - y show.

It takes nine men to make a side,
Who play upon the square,
The Umpire settles all disputes,
And occupies the chair.
The Scorer keeps the "tally" list,
And with a watchful eye,
The Captains send the men around
To catch it on the "Fly."
Chorus

Then when a challenge game is played –
All dressed in bright array,
They march to meet a brother club,
And have gala day.
'Tis then the neighbors gather 'round,
Excitement runs on high,
For both are bound to beat and win
In catching on the "Fly."
Chorus

The Pitcher sends the ball to bat
While standing on the square.
The Catcher just behind "Home Base"
Must catch it foul or fair.
The Fielders – Centre, Right and Left
Are gazing at the sky,
All watching for the ball to come,
To catch it on the "Fly."
Chorus

Throughout the East, throughout the West,
The game is all the rage,
And many a game is often played
Before the wise and sage.
It puts the vim right into a man –
'Twill raise his spirits high,
And make him live to good old age
To catch it on the "Fly."
Chorus

HURRAH FOR OUR NATIONAL GAME
1869

On July 28, 1841, the body of 21-year-old Mary Rogers was pulled from the Hudson River just offshore from the Elysian Fields, a popular outdoor recreational area in Hoboken, New Jersey, just across the river from lower Manhattan. She was known in New York City as "the Beautiful Cigar Girl" because of her comely appearance and her employment in a popular cigar emporium, to which men would flock in the hopes of catching her eye. The mysterious circumstances regarding her apparent murder excited the interest of the press and the public on both sides of the Hudson. Among those who attempted (unsuccessfully, as it turned out) to solve the crime was none other than Edgar Allen Poe, who semi-fictionalized the affair in his tale "The Mystery of Marie Rogêt." Here again, as mentioned in "Catch It on the Fly," Poe's literary trajectory improbably intersected with baseball—for the first baseball game played under "modern rules," as drawn up by Alexander J. Cartwright, took place on June 19, 1846 at the Elysian Fields (the New Yorkers beat the Knickerbockers 23-1 in four innings).

The year 1869, when "Hurrah for Our National Game" was composed, witnessed a number of significant events in the history of baseball. The Cincinnati Red Stockings became the first professional club. They marked this occasion in their opening game on May 4 by crushing the amateur Great Westerns 45-9. They even had a theme song, which started out well enough, but concluded rather weakly:

> We are a band of baseball players
>   from Cincinnati city.
> We come to toss the ball around,
> and sing to you our ditty.
> And if you listen to the song
>   we are about to sing,
> We'll tell you all about baseball
>   and make the welkin ring.
> The ladies want to know
> Who are those gallant men
> In stockings red,
> They'd like to know.

On June 26, President Ulysses S. Grant honored the Red Stockings with an invitation to the White House. On September 18, the all-black Philadelphia Pythians (who had been refused membership in the National Association) defeated the all-white City Items 27-17 in an exhibition game. It was the first time that an all-black team played an all-white team. All of these events happened in 1869.

In 1871, the Reds moved to Boston and the Boston Red Stockings were born. Walter Neville, the composer of "Hurrah for Our National Game," was a member of the Olympic Base Ball Club of New York, one of over 100 teams based in that city. There is an anthem-like quality to the song, with its call to "Conscience" (with a capital C) while playing our "National Game. "

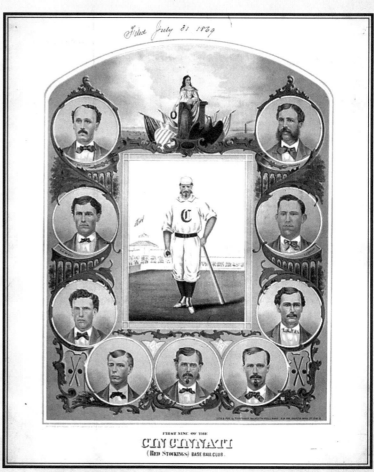

The first nine of the Cincinnati Red Stockings, ca. 1869.

Respectfully Dedicated
TO ALL WHO

Hurrah For Our National Game.

WRITTEN & COMPOSED BY

WALTER NEVILLE

OF THE OLYMPIC B. B. CLUB OF NEW YORK.

NEW YORK.
Published by C. H. DITSON & CO. 711 Broadway

J. Church Jr. Cinn.
J. C. Haynes & Co. Boston

Boston.
O. DITSON & CO.

C. W. A. Trumpler, Phil.ᵃ
Lyon & Healy, Chicago.

HURRAH FOR OUR NATIONAL GAME

Words and Music by
Walter Neville

1. Hur - rah for our game, our Na - tion - al. Game, There's__ health in its ev - 'ry

bound. A thrill of de - light in its ve - ry name, A

joy in its sim - ple sound. It lends new__ strength to our har - dy__ race, And its

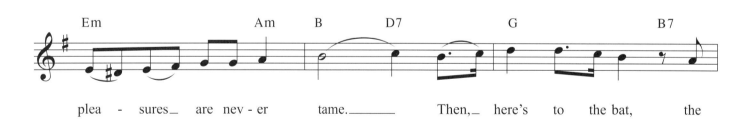

plea - sures__ are nev - er tame._____ Then,__ here's to the bat, the

ball and the base: Hur - rah for our Na - tion - al Game._____

Chorus

Then hur-rah for our Na-tion-al Game, Hur-rah, here's a cheer for its well-earned fame. Suc - cess to it ev - er, Hur - rah, Hur - rah, Hur - rah for our Na - tion - al Game.

The timid lament o'er such dangerous fun,
And groan at "that terrible ball."
The lazy ones shrink from "making a run,"
And cowards are fearing a fall.
 But give us the dash of a strong "home strike,"
 And we laugh such weak folly to shame.
 Take all of the other sports and do what you like,
 But leave us our National Game.
Chorus

The Gamester may boast of the pleasures of play,
The Billiardist brag of his cue,
The Horse Jockey gabble of next racing day,
The Yachtsman discourse of the blue.
 The patrons of Racket feast on its joys,
 Whilst Cricket it's lovers inflame.
 Croquet's very well for young ladies and boys,
 But give us our National Game.
Chorus

Now toss for the innings, the bases are down,
Outsiders go into the field.
The scorer with tallies successes will crown,
As each striker the "willow" doth wield.
 The Captains assign each player his place,
 The Umpire his rulings will name.
 To all their decisions submit with good grace.
 As required by our National Game.
Chorus

And thus 'tis in life, each one has a post,
Assigned by the Captain of all.
While the great Umpire "Conscience" is guiding the host,
Take heed that we list to his call.
 May no "base play" be ours, may our record be bright,
 With no "foul deeds" our "clean score" to shame.
 Let us play life's game nobly, respecting the right,
 As we do in out National Game.
Chorus

LORD BALTIMORE'S NINE
1872

Before there were the Baltimore Orioles, there were the Baltimore Canaries of the National Association. Their brief existence lasted from 1872 to 1874. They played in Newington Park; their stadium has since vanished without a trace. Clinton S. Birch set the lyrics to the well-known tune of the day, "Down in a Coal Mine," which had been composed in 1872 by popular comedian and songwriter J. B. Geoghegan. It was published in a broadside (without music).

Tobacco card, ca. 1867.

LORD BALTIMORE'S NINE.

Air- Down in a Coal Mine.

We are a jovial Base Ball Club,
  Our hearts are light and free,
And though we meet with some defeats,
  Oft gain the victory.
Give us fair play, and win or lose,
  We'll never make a muss,
But be content and act like men,
  Yes, that's the style for us.

CHORUS·

Out at the Newington Park,
  On the Base Ball ground,
When in earnest contest
  Our gallant Nine are found,
Struggling with their rivals,
  For victory and renown,
Out at the Newington Park,
  On the Base Ball ground:

Of all the manly games in vogue,
  Enumerate them all,
There's none you'll find that can compare
  With that known as Base Ball.
'Tis jolly fun when on the run,
  Or when with eagle eye.
You watch your adversary's ball,
  And take it on the fly.

We make no boasts, but stand resolved
  To win ourselves a name,
And we will do the best we can
  To merit all we claim.
We're not afraid of rival clubs,
  We'll meet them anywhere,
And when then choose to play us here
  We'll act upon the square.

Clinton S. Birch,

LORD BALTIMORE'S NINE

Words by
Clinton S. Birch

Music by
J. B. Geoghegan

We are a jov-ial Base Ball Club, Our hearts are light and free, And

though we meet with some de-feats, Oft gain the vic - to - ry. Give

us fair play, and win or lose, We'll nev - er make a muss, But

be con-tent and act like men, Yes, that's the __ style for us.

Chorus

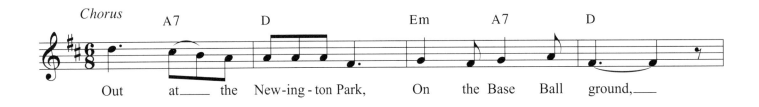

Out at __ the New-ing-ton Park, On the Base Ball ground, __

When in earn - est con - test Our gal - lant Nine are found, __

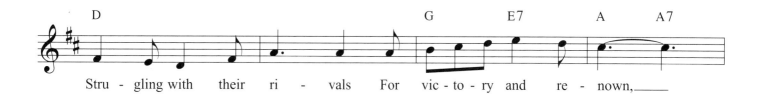

Stru - gling with their ri - vals For vic - to - ry and re - nown,___

Out at___ the New-ing - ton Park, On the Base Ball ground.___

Of all the manly games in vogue,
Enumerate them all,
There's none you'll find that can compare
With that known as Base Ball.
'Tis jolly fun when on the run,
Or when with eagle eye,
You watch your adversary's ball,
And take it on the fly.
Chorus

We make no boasts, but stand resolved
To win ourselves a name,
And we will do the best we can,
To merit the aclaim.
We're not afraid of rival clubs,
We'll meet them anywhere,
And when they choose to play us,
We'll play them on the square.
Chorus

THE BASE BALL SONG
1874

William John Bullock was a multi-faceted British theatrical producer, composer and performer on the guitar who introduced his "blackface minstrel" marionette show to American audiences in 1872. His British-influenced musical and literary style is abundantly evident in this 1874 composition. With its references to "the sweet green fields of home," "peer and peasant" and "innings" (a cricket term), the song sounds more like Merrie Olde England than Mudville. "Benedicts" in verse 3 refers to Benedick, the confident bachelor in Shakespeare's "Much Ado About Nothing," who courts and finally marries Beatrice. By extension, a "benedict" is a newly married man—especially one who has long been a bachelor. The connection between "prowess in the field" (verse 2) of sport and affairs of the heart is thus firmly established. There is a discrepancy with the title of this song, between what was printed on the cover of the sheet music ("Base Ball Song") and what appears on the first page of the music ("The Base Ball").

Cricket match between the All England Eleven and the United States Twenty-Two, 1859.

Baseball match at the Elysian Fields, Hoboken, ca. 1859.

To the BASE BALL CLUBS,
Of the United States.

Base Ball Song

Words & Music by

W. J. BULLOCK,

Sole proprietor of

Bullock's Royal Marionettes.

BOSTON.
OLIVER DITSON & Cº 277 WASHINGTON Sᵀ
N. YORK, C. H. DITSON & Cº

Chicago
Lyon & Healy

Cinn.
J. Church & Co.

Boston
J. C. Haynes & Co.

Philᵃ
Lee & Walker

THE BASE BALL SONG

Words and Music by
W. J. Bullock

Moderato

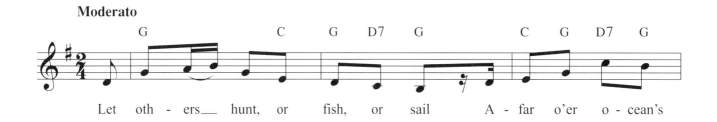

Let oth - ers__ hunt, or fish, or sail A - far o'er o - cean's

foam; Give me the__ game that's played a - mong The sweet green__ fields of

home. The Bas - es pitch on a le - vel__ spot, Be - neath a smil - ing__

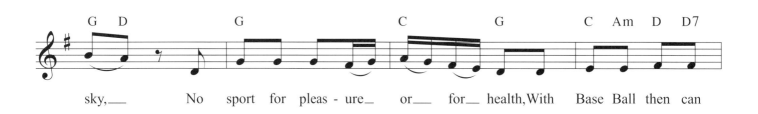

sky,__ No sport for pleas - ure__ or__ for__ health, With Base Ball then can

vie,__ With Base_ Ball then can vie. Then__ take the bat and the

ball in hand, Let the um - pire sing out "play." For Base Ball is a

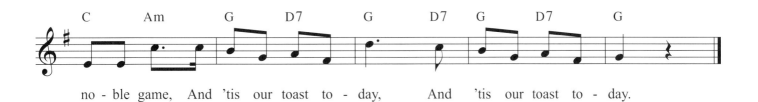

no - ble game, And 'tis our toast to - day, And 'tis our toast to - day.

For peer and peasant, man and boy,
This game to none can yield.
Both rich and poor delight to show
Their prowess in the field.
Then join your voices, give three cheers
For bases, bat and ball;
Success to our B.B. Club –
Prosperity to all,
Prosperity to all
Chorus

Ye Benedicts, who the "match have played,"
No doubt you'll say you've won
A darling wife, an angel quite —
If so, your part's well done.
But you, ye single Base Ball men
Can't estimate your winnings.
But I hope when the question you have pop'd,
You'll have a successful "innings,"
You'll have a successful "innings."
Chorus

TALLY ONE FOR ME
1877

Among the other songs that John T. Rutledge composed in 1877 were the sentimental "Little Darling, Never Trust Me" and "The Mill Will Never Grind with the Water that Has Passed."

His sentimental nature extended to the world of baseball, easily moving from "tallying" on the field to "tallying" off the field. Evidently, as early as 1877, diamonds were a girl's best friend.

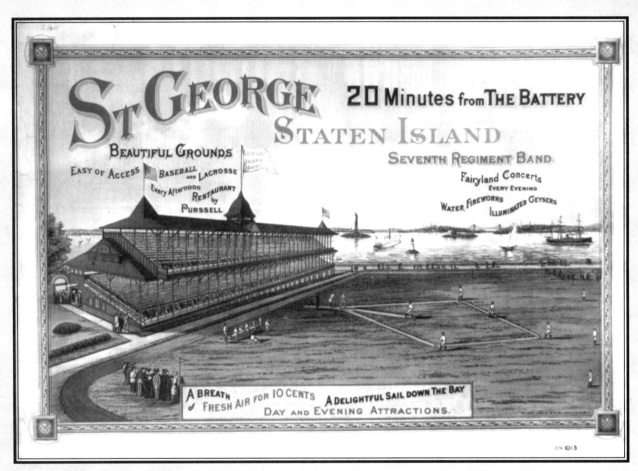

Advertisement with a baseball game in progress, ca. 1886.

TALLY ONE FOR ME

Words and Music by
John T. Rutledge

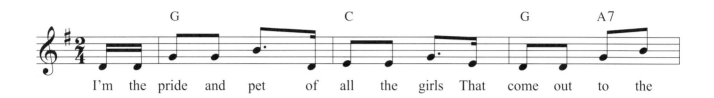

I'm the pride and pet of all the girls That come out to the

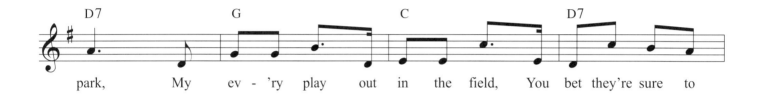

park, My ev - 'ry play out in the field, You bet they're sure to

mark. And when you see them smil - ing, And their hands go pit - a - pat, Just

mark it down, For num - ber one is go - ing to the bat.

Chorus

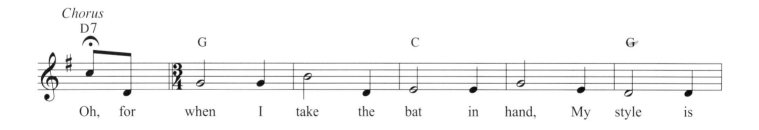

Oh, for when I take the bat in hand, My style is

sure and free;_____ Just put your mon - ey on my

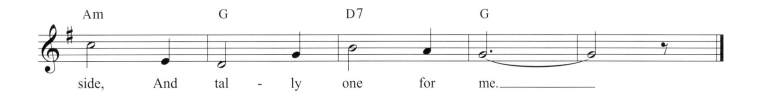

side, And tal - ly one for me._____

I never knock the ball up high,
Or even make it bound,
But always send it whizzing,
Cutting daisies on the bround.
I always make a clean base hit,
And go around, you see –
And that's the reason why I say,
Just tally one for me.
Chorus

I soon will stop my "balling,"
For my heart is led astray.
'Twas stolen by a nice young girl,
By her exquisite play.
And after we are married,
Why, I hope hope you'll come to see
The "tally" I have made for life –
And mark one down for me.
Chorus

OUR NOBLE GIANT NINE!
1889

Monroe Rosenfeld's compositions, such as "With All Her Faults I Love Her Still" (1888), helped set the musical tone for the Gilded Age of the 1880s and '90s. In 1888 and 1889, the N.Y. Giants won the World Series; in '88 against the St. Louis Browns, in '89 against the Brooklyn Bridegrooms. People began calling the New York team the "Giants" as a tribute to their victories and the name stuck. Rosenfeld, sensing a good image for a song, stepped right up to the plate.

Tobacco cards featuring players from New York (left) and St. Louis (right), ca. 1889.

OUR NOBLE GIANT NINE!

Words and Music by
Monroe H. Rosenfeld

Cheers for the boys who have won it, The pen-nant of our pride;

Brave-ly in man-y a bat-tle, They've strug-gled side by side.

Now with the lau-rels of vic-t'ry, Their gal-lant brows we twine, The

first on the dia-mond field of fame: That no-ble Gi-ant nine!

Chorus

For they're our gal-lant cham-pions, The har-dy and the true: Long

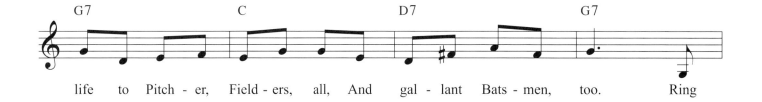

life to Pitch-er, Field-ers, all, And gal-lant Bats-men, too. Ring

out their prais - es to the skies, Their fame shall ev - er shine. May

home - runs still the rec - ord fill, Of our no - ble Gi - ant nine!

Brave are the hearts that have struggled
To keep the record bright;
Hail to the conquerng heroes,
The boys of nerve and might.
Many a "curve" that has startled,
 Has marked their play as fine.
We'll greet them with a thousand cheers:
Our noble Giant nine!
Chorus

First on the field of the diamond,
To them we doff our hat;
This be forever their record:
The Kings of Ball and Bat.
Cheers for the Champion players,
Unsullied be their shrine.
Praise for the heroes of our land:
Our gallant Giant nine!
Chorus

STEAL! SLIDE! ANYWAY!
1889

From 1883 to 1888, the New York Giants played in Polo Grounds 1, which was located at the northern end of Central Park. When the city confiscated the property, they moved briefly (April 29 to June 14, 1889) to St. Georges Grounds on Staten Island before moving into their new home, Polo Grounds 2 in Coogan's Hollow (also known as Coogan's Bluff), between 155th and 157th Streets in Manhattan. By 1891, having outgrown the seating capacity there, they moved to yet another, larger Polo Grounds a few blocks further north.

The Giants won the World Series in 1888 and 1889. Notable players include Johnny Ward, who played shortstop from 1885 to 1889, and pitcher Tim Keefe whose W-L record in '88 was 35-12; in '89, it was 28-13. Keefe was inducted into the Hall of Fame in 1964. Jim ("Truthful Jim") Murtrie managed the Giants. Their record in '88 was 84-47; 83-43 in '89. Cap Anson played first base for the rival Chicago Colts. His lifetime batting average was .333. And how about those padded trousers!

Boston and New York players on opening day at the Polo Grounds, 1886.

Dedicated to
The N.Y. Base Ball Club.

Steal! Slide! Anyway!

WORDS BY VIRGINIA DUNCAN.

MUSIC BY JAMES MASCOTTE.

NEW YORK.,
PUBLISHED BY N. WEINSTEIN, 24 WEST 23d ST.

STEAL! SLIDE! ANYWAY!

Words by
Virgina Duncan

Music by
James Mascotte

Boston men the "sluggers" are!
"Anson's colts" may kick!
Let them have their little game,
We will make them sick!
Heading all the others,
We are "in the swim."
Bobbing up serenely,
Led by "Truthful Jim!"
Chorus

Ev'ry man's the strongest link
In this flawless chain!
Wait awhile, and you will see,
Pennant ours again!
Give the other nines chance,
Let them win a game.
It will keep their courage up,
We'll get there all the same.
Chorus

Tim Keefe, ca. 1887.

John Ward, ca. 1887.

Baseball Pants.

Baseball Pants are made to order. **Send cash with the order.** All our baseball pants are **heavily padded and quilted and come with elastic bottom.** When ordering, give waist and length measure. Pants should go below the knee, about 4 to 6 inches.

NOTICE—Many players are using football pants for baseball games, claiming they are stronger though they don't look quite as well.

No. 6R7066 Best Athletic Worsted Flannel, in white, navy blue, maroon and gray colors. Give measurement. Per pair....**$2.75**

No. 6R7067 Medium Grade Athletic Worsted Flannel, in navy blue, maroon or pearl gray colors. Give measurement. Per pair.**$2.00**

No. 6R7068 Best Cotton Athletic Fabric, in blue gray or mixed gray colors. Give measurement. Per pair.................**$1.50**

No. 6R7069 Ordinary Cotton Fabric, in brown, blue or white color only. Give measurement. Per pair..(If by mail, postage extra, 25c)...**$1.25**

Padded trousers from Sears catalog, ca. 1902.

Cap Anson, ca. 1887.

FINNEGAN, THE UMPIRE
1890

This is a bit of pure nonsense. We're not sure why Finnegan, the umpire, "swung his bat." We're not sure what's going on between O'Mara "on first base" and the shortstop, and not to mention what a bat is doing in "centre field."

What we do get here is the stereotyped Irish "Mick," who brought howls of laughter from the vaudeville audiences of the period. After hitting a home run with "Our Noble Giant Nine," Rosenfeld struck out with this one.

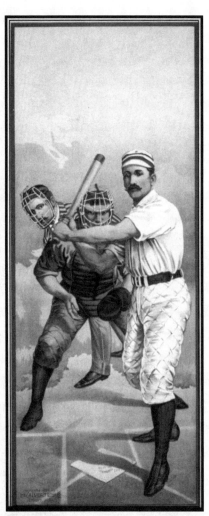

Lithograph, ca. 1895.

Supplement to No. 772 of THE BOYS OF NEW YORK.

FINNEGAN THE UMPIRE
BY MONROE H. ROSENFELD.

FINNEGAN, THE UMPIRE

Words and Music by
Monroe H. Rosenfeld

Tempo di Schottische

Mi-chael Fin - ne-gan one day, when the boys be-gan to play, Was

dressed as fine as an - y duke or lord; He___ wore a new silk hat, and an

el - e-gant cra-vat, And he swung his bat just like a mar-shall's sword.___ 'Twas O'-

Ma-ra on first base, he had just be-gun to chase, When the short-stop sent the ball in with a

howl; But 'twas such a splen-did curve, that Fin'-gan lost his nerve, And be-

fore he caught his breath he yelled out "Foul!"___ One strike, two strikes, the

third one knocked him out. "You're off your base, go hide your face!" the

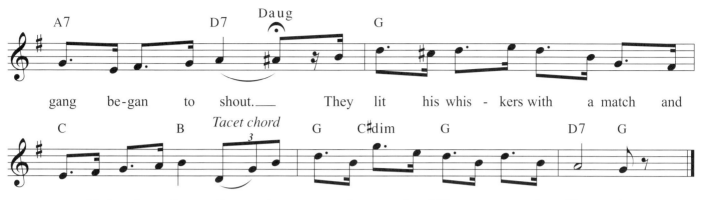

gang be-gan to shout.___ They lit his whis - kers with a match and

set his beard a-fire, Sure,_ they near - ly mur - dered Fin - ne-gan, the Um - pire.

Then Duffy took the bat,
And he knew where he was at,
He sent a daisy cutter whizzing by;
And intent to see the play,
Fin'gan got into the way,
And it landed in the middle of his eye.
Then for "judgement" someone called,
And a dozen 'round him bawled,
"Let's tie his bloomin' whiskers to his hair."
And his heart began to quake,
And his knees began to shake,
And to satisfy the gang he yelled out, "Fair"
Chorus

In the melee that occured
Fin'gan couldn't say a word,
Tho' he tried to smile a sickly giggle, when
From the bat in centre field,
A ball his nozzle peeled,
And struck him squarely in the abdomen.
Yet they saw he wasn't dead,
So they stood him on his head,
And for his whiskers quick they made a dive;
When with one accord the crowd
Shouted out in glee aloud,
"Oh! hurry up and roast the Mick alive!"
Chorus

When he got in town that night,
Mickey was an awful sight,
He looked as if he'd struck a train of cars.
And his tall and shiny hat
Looked just like a baseball bat,
And his whiskers dangled like a flag of stars.
Now he never reads the score,
To the "diamond" goes no more,
Mention "umpire." if you want to hear him growl.
T'other day he said to me,
"Why, they'll slaughter you," says he,
"No matter if you sing out Fair or Foul."
Chorus

McGUFFIN'S HOME RUN
COMIC SONG AND CHORUS
1891

Composer Gussie Lord Davis's (1863–1899) greatest hit was the 1896 tearjerker "In the Baggage Car Ahead," a sad tale of a child weeping aboard a railroad train because his mother is in a coffin "in the baggage car ahead." True to the spirit of the times, five years earlier he set to music Bert Norman's "Irish" lyrics—complete with (in addition to the mythical "McGuffin") a "Pat McCann," a "Katie Duffy" and the all-purpose "begorra." Davis, born in Ohio during the Civil War, was one of the late-19th century's first commercially successful African-American songwriters and was one of the charter members of Tin Pan Alley, which came into being in New York in 1885. Among his contemporaries were Scott Joplin and W. C. Handy.

Philadelphia Athletic players on the field with a marching band, 1908.

To Frank McMahon, Washington, D.C.

McGUFFIN'S HOME RUN

Comic Song:

WORDS BY

Bert. C. Norman,

MUSIC BY

GUSSIE L. DAVIS.

NEW-YORK:

Willis Woodward & Co.,

842 & 844 BROADWAY.

Copyright MDCCCXCI by Willis Woodward & Co.

McGUFFIN'S HOME RUN
COMIC SONG AND CHORUS

Words by
Bert C. Norman

Music by
Gussie L. Davis

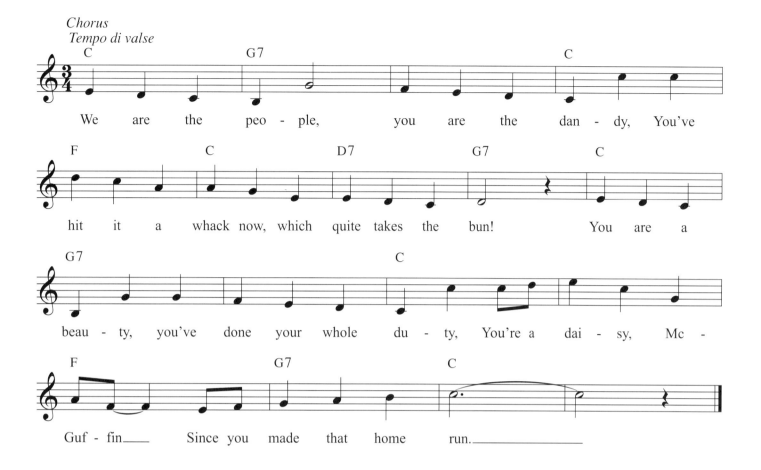

We are the peo - ple, you are the dan - dy, You've hit it a whack now, which quite takes the bun! You are a beau - ty, you've done your whole du - ty, You're a dai - sy, Mc - Guf - fin___ Since you made that home run.___

Pat McCann stepped up to me then,
Says he, "Sure you're a King.
To see you swipe that baseball
Was enough to make one sing!
Come, boys, a tiger* we'll give him,
Or, sure, your heads he'll break.
And when he dies, begorra,
We'll give him a rousng wake!"
I went to get some beer to drink,
And find a cooler place.
When 'pon me soul, a bo[u]quet
Struck me squarely in the face!
I stood the situation,
Like an other man,
When Katie Duffy whispered
As she tapped me with her fan:
Chorus

*An additional cheer including the word "tiger" at the end of a round of cheering.

O'GRADY AT THE GAME
1891

O' Grady was yet another stereotyped "Irish" comic music hall figure so dear to late 19th-century audiences. Combining an "O'Grady" with baseball and hi-jinks, during and after the game, was a sure-fire combination guaranteed to please.

This tobacco card, ca. 1886, features Tony Mullane who was born in Ireland and pitched from 1881 to 1894. His lifetime ERA was 3.05.

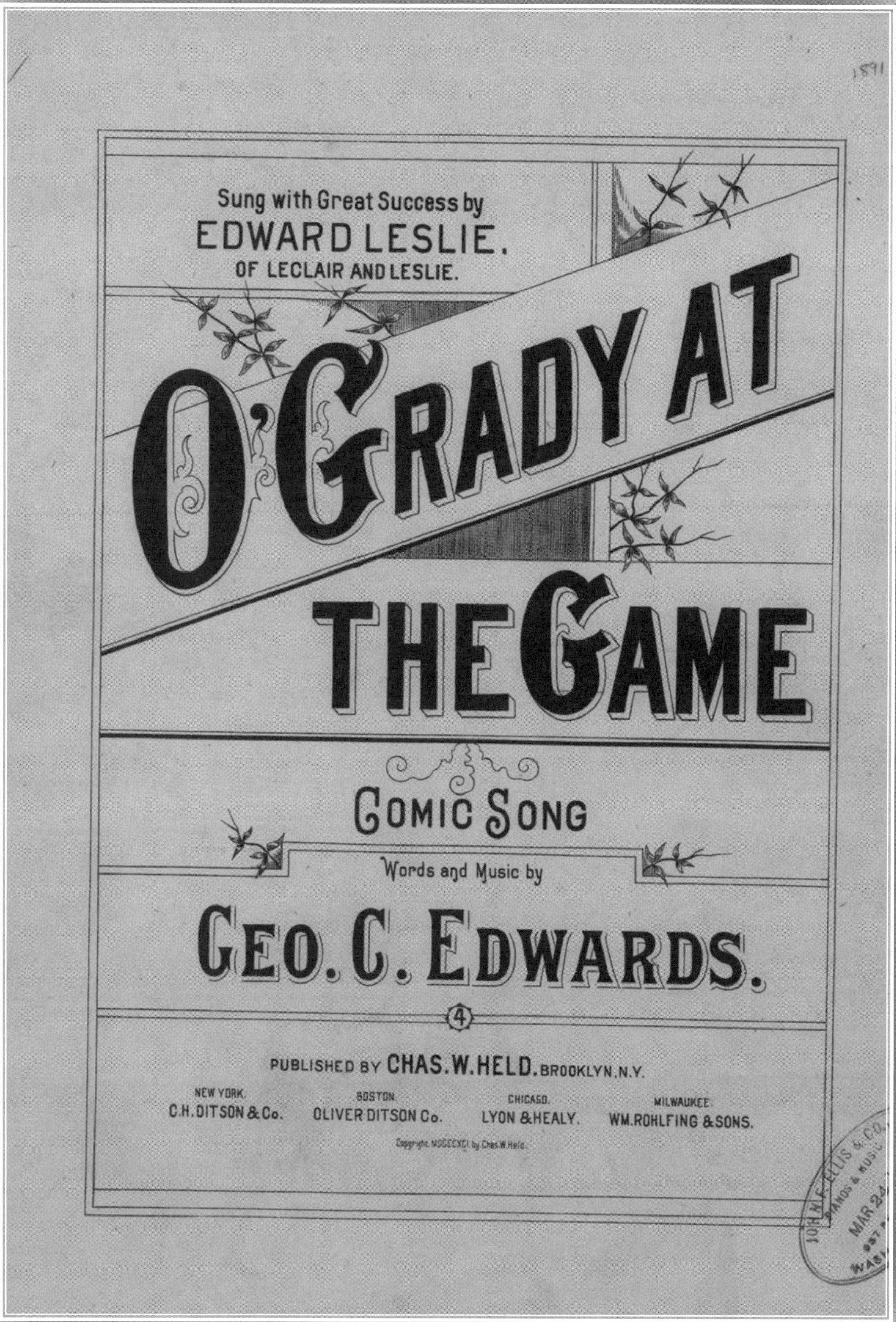

Sung with Great Success by
EDWARD LESLIE.
OF LECLAIR AND LESLIE.

O'GRADY AT THE GAME

COMIC SONG

Words and Music by

GEO. C. EDWARDS.

④

PUBLISHED BY **CHAS. W. HELD.** BROOKLYN, N.Y.

NEW YORK.	BOSTON.	CHICAGO.	MILWAUKEE.
C. H. DITSON & Co.	OLIVER DITSON Co.	LYON & HEALY.	WM. ROHLFING & SONS.

Copyright, MDCCCXCI by Chas. W. Held.

O'GRADY AT THE GAME

Words and Music by
George C. Edwards

'Twas in the seventh inning and the game it was a tie,
O'Grady had ten dollars bet and felt as if he'd die.
Then Mulligan came in the bat, which made O'Grady howl.
His "fly" went in a chicken coop, the umpire whisper'd foul.
The players then came from the field, the umpire got it rough
O'Grady stood up like a man, and gave him lots of "guff."
And when the game came to an end the score stood ten to three,
Then old O'Grady, Mc and I went off upon a spree.
Chorus

We went down to Mike Murphy's and began on lager beer.
In less time than I felt it we were feeling mighty queer.
Mc turned on poor O'Grady and he threw him in the sink.
He thought he was a "Fasset"* or the famous mising link.
'Twas bad for poor O'Grady, sure, the day he saw that game.
His clothes they were in tatters and his arms and legs were lame.
He swore at me in English and he curs'd the game in French,
And not until next season will you see him on the bench.
Chorus

* Faucet

TOLD BETWEEN TICKS
1891

Growing up in the Bronx as a Brooklyn Dodger fan (!), the mellifluous radio voice of Red Barber was the link to my beloved Bums. When they played their home games in Ebbets field, I could visualize Red, high in the "catbird seat," calling the play-by-play. The sounds of the rabid fans added to the excitement, but when the team played on the road all that could be heard (besides Red's voice) was the clicking of the ticker tape in the studio. There were no live broadcasts of the away games, but Red managed to convey all the excitement of those faraway encounters: "Musial hits a scorcher to short...Pee Wee Reese scoops it up on a short hop and fires it to Dixie Walker...Out at

first!...A bang-bang play!" How did he know it was a scorcher? How did he know it was a short hop and a bang-bang play? I believed every word he said. It was only years later that I learned that those "ticks" just gave the bare essentials: "Grounder to short. Out at first," or some such laconic telegraphese. Red was making it all up "between the ticks." But it didn't matter then, and it doesn't matter now.

Charlie Reed, a well-known singer and actor, introduced "Told Between Ticks" in the Reed and Collier production of "Hoss and Hoss" at the Hollis Street Theater in Boston in November, 1891.

Illustration of a ticker-tape parade, ca. 1888.

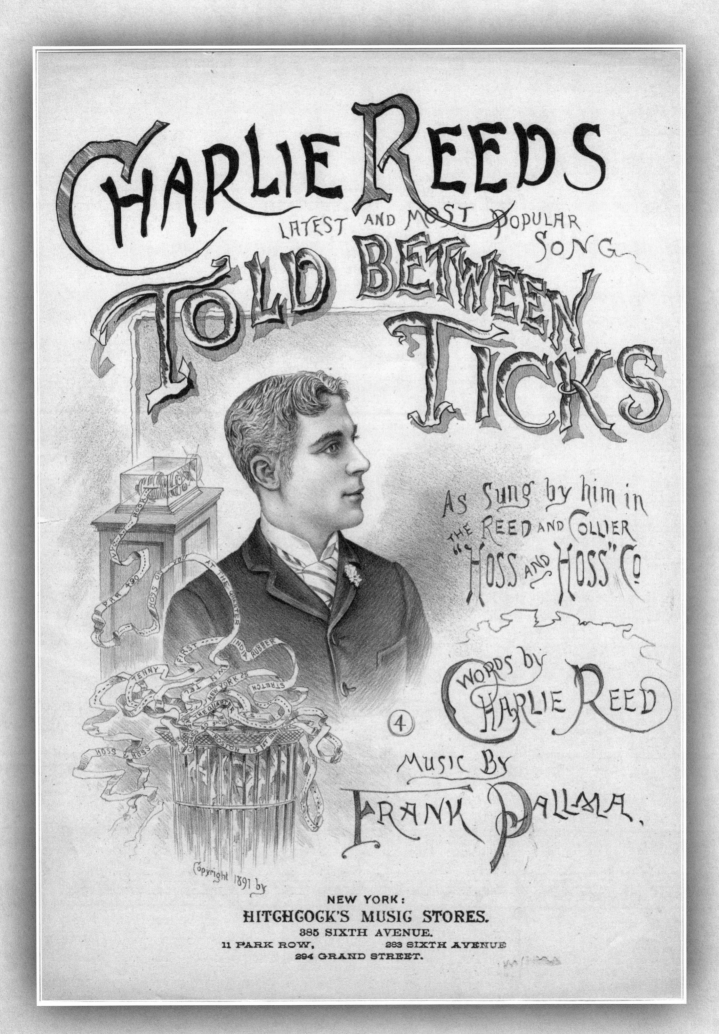

TOLD BETWEEN THE TICKS

Words by
Charlie Reed

Music by
Frank Pallma

Up - on this nar - row bit of tape, That I am read - ing now Some

fun - ny bits of news ap - pear, Of course, that you'll al - low. There's

news from Sheeps-head, Con - ey Isle And Mor - ris Park as well. And

how the ra - ces have been run, This lit - tle tape will tell.

Here's a man who's called cra - zy, There's one called a Dai - sy, An -

oth - er one called at a quar - ter past six. Here's a man called at Po - ker, By a

man with a Jo - ker, And all of this news is told between ticks.

What's this I see, that troubles me,
I cannot make it out,
A man is called a German now,
Who orders Saurkraut.
The Broadway cable cars, it says,
 Are running on a track.
You drop a nickel in the slot,
And never get it back.
Here's some news from Australia,
About a big failure,
And news from Hong Kong of Chinese up to tricks.
Here's news from Toronto,
It's a good place to run to,
And all of this news is told between ticks.
Chorus

The latest from the Base Ball grounds;
The catcher caught a catch.
The Pitcher pitch'd a Pitcher
At this champion Base Ball match.
The first Base took the second Base
To third Base, where they met.
And made a short stop at the home,
And sang a Jay Quartette.
Here's news from the Right Field,
Here's news from the Left Field.
Here's news from the Centre Field up to his tricks.
Here's news from the umpire,
Who is often called Liar,
And all of this news is told between ticks.
Chorus

OUR NATIONAL GAME
1894

It is interesting to note that "our sweethearts fair" (verse 2) watched the game from the comfort of a "carry-all"—an omnibus with benches running the length of the carriage. The word is derived from the French *cariole*, a small, open two-wheeled vehicle. In its Americanized pronunciation, it came to describe a larger conveyance (in effect, a "carry-all").

When the crowd gathers 'round, in verse 3, to "guy" the pitcher, they are jeering him. This time, the term is derived from British slang—the "guy" in question being Guy Fawkes, who unsuccessfully attempted blow up Parliament on November 5, 1605. On Guy Fawkes Day (Nov. 5), an effigy of Fawkes is paraded through the streets of London, where he is "guyed" by the population.

The 12 captains of the National League, ca. 1895.

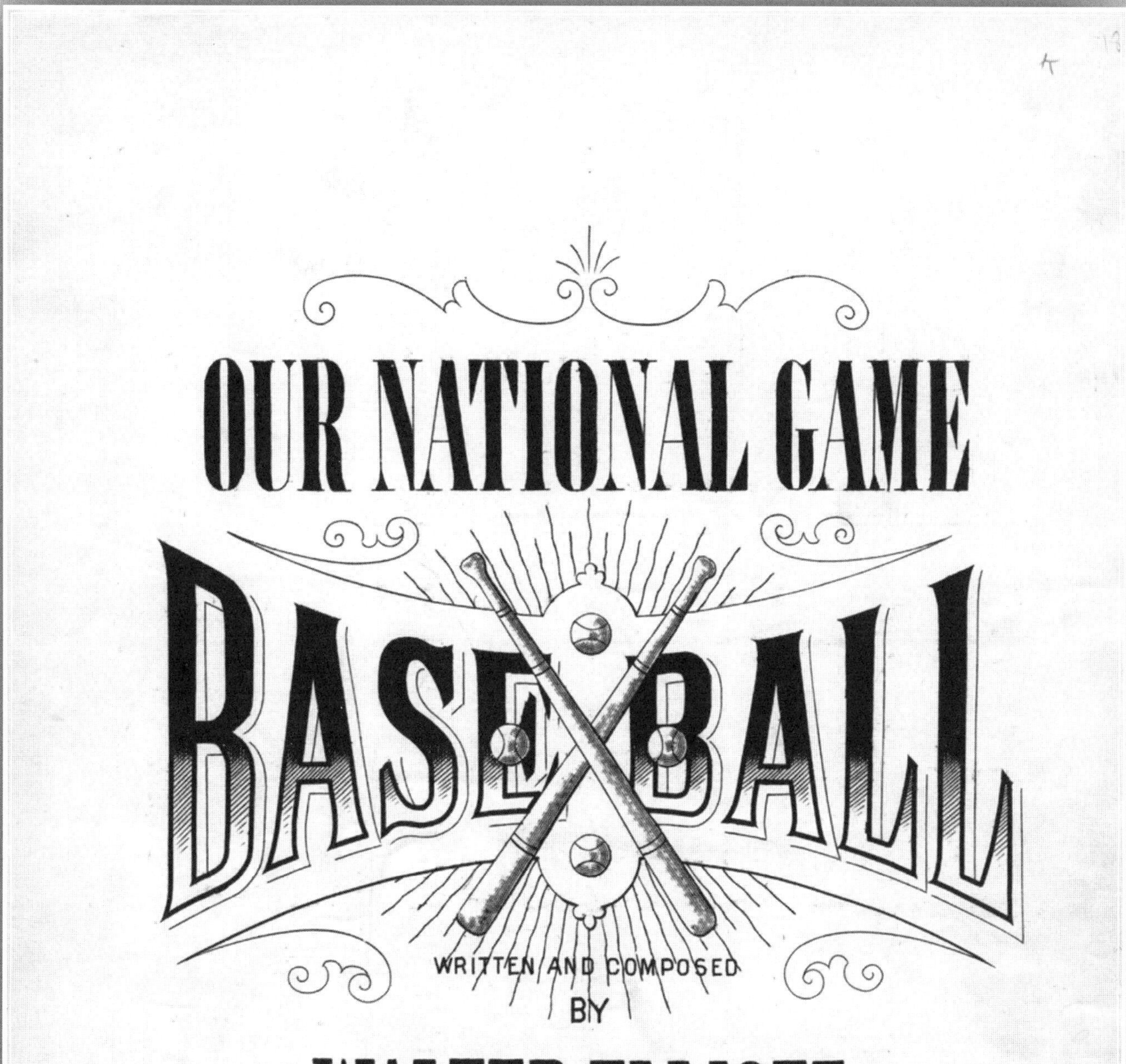

OUR NATIONAL GAME

BASE BALL

WRITTEN AND COMPOSED

BY

WALTER ELLIOTT.

④

OUR NATIONAL GAME

Words and Music by
Walter Elliott

Allegro moderato

Some fel-lows boast what games they have, and what fun they do en-joy. While oth-ers can not_ find a game their lei-sure to em-ploy; But I know one which you all know, and one that beats them all, There's noth-ing, boys, cre-ates such joys, as the game of games, base-ball.

Chorus
Valse tempo

Play-ing at ball, play-ing at ball. Watch-ing with pleas-ure which way goes the ball._____ Play-ing at ball, play-ing at

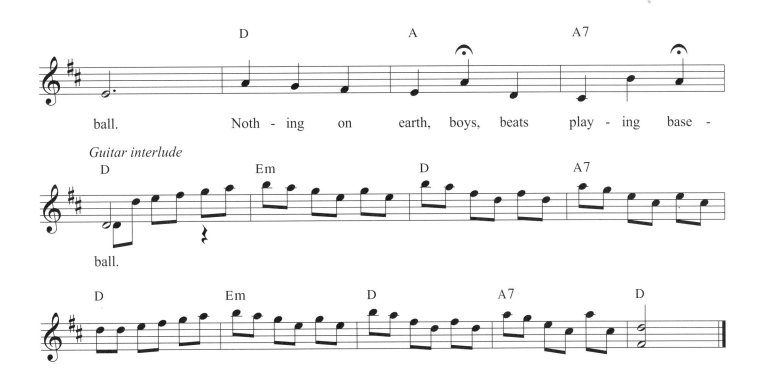

ball.   Noth - ing   on   earth, boys, beats   play - ing   base -

Guitar interlude

ball.

America's national game it is, played by both young and old,
And sports in it delight to bet their silver, bills and gold;
Our sweethearts fair, its joys do share, as they watch from the carry-all,
And laugh and shout as the ball flies out, for they love the game baseball.
Chorus

Of course, a crowd is gathered 'round as the pitcher they do "guy,"
As the batsman hits the ball so swift, and sends it to the sky;
But O, the fun as he "home" doth run, as they wait for the ball to fall,
And the catcher shouts, "There are two outs!" Come there do play baseball.
Chorus

With interest we watch the game, and our favorites we do cheer,
As the game they win, 'midst the roar and din, coming from the field so clear;
To our homes we go with hearts aglow with the sport well known to all,
The game of games, our joy, our pride, our national game, baseball.
Chorus

WHO WOULD DOUBT THAT I'M A MAN?
1895

What we have here is not a baseball song but a baseball aria. It comes from an operetta entitled *The Mormons*, and is sung by a woman who, dressed in a man's baseball uniform, outhits, outruns, outcatches and generally outplays her male counterparts. The Mormon Church Historical Library has no copy of this work in its files, but according to Jeff Johnson, a research archivist at the Latter Day Saints Archives in Salt Lake City: "During this time, there was a lot of 'making fun' of the Mormons, and I am thinking that this might be in that category."

Women who dressed as men for various reasons are not uncommon in operas and folksongs: Leonora disguised as Fidelio in Beethoven's opera *Fidelio*, seeks to find her imprisoned husband; Gilda in *Rigoletto*, similarly disguised, sacrifices herself to save the life of her erstwhile low-life lover, the Duke of Mantua—to name but two.

In the English folksong "William Taylor," the motive of the young woman is quite different from that of her operatic sisters. Taylor sails off before their wedding, and…

> *She dressed up in a man's apparel,*
> *Man's apparel she put on,*
> *And she followed her true lover,*
> *For to find him she is gone.*

But when she catches up with him, she finds him "walking with a lady gay."

> *Sword and pistol then she ordered*
> *To be brought at her command,*
> *And she shot her true love William,*
> *With the bride at his right hand.*

Then there is the "Handsome Cabin Boy," whose story turns out quite differently.

> *'Tis of a handsome female,*
> *As you may understand,*
> *Her mind being bent on*
> *   rambling unto some foreign land,*
> *She dressed herself in sailor's clothes,*
> *Or so it does appear,*
> *And hired with our captain,*
> *To serve him for a year.*

But the captain "found out the secret of the handsome cabin boy," with predictable results. By the time the ship reached the Bay of Biscay,

> *…The doctor come a-running,*
> *And smiled at the fun,*
> *To think a sailor lad should have*
> *A daughter or a son.*

Returning to baseball…

By the time *The Mormons* was written in 1895, the first women's baseball team had been organized in Vassar College in 1886. In 1867, a group of black women in Philadelphia formed the first professional women's team, the Dolly Vardens. On September 11, 1875 in Springfield, Illinois, the "Blondes" played the "Brunettes" before a paying crowd. The 1890s saw the rise of women's baseball teams outfitted in loose-fitting trousers designed by Suffragist Amelia Bloomer. The Bloomer Girls baseball teams (as they were called) often played (and beat) men's teams. Judging by the sheet music cover of "Who Would Doubt That I'm a Man?," our heroine is a Bloomer Girl.

DEDICATED TO
THE NEW WOMAN.

BASE BALL SONG

SPECIALLY
ADAPTED FROM THE COMIC OPERA
"THE MORMONS",
GREATEST HIT OF THE SEASON.

WHO WOULD DOUBT THAT I'M A MAN?

"A HIT
A VERY PALPABLE HIT, ⑤
HAMLET.

PUBLISHED BY
WEIDIG AND **COMPANY**
◦ CINCINNATI ◦

WHO WOULD DOUBT THAT I'M A MAN?

Words by
M. S.

Music by
A. F. Groebl

*"No curveballs, please. Just put it over the plate."

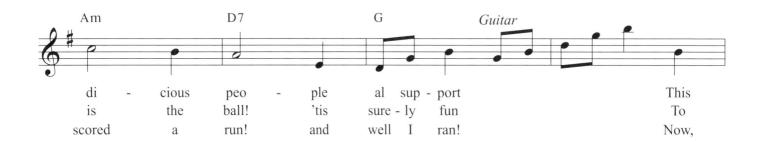

di - cious peo - ple al sup - port This
is the ball! 'tis sure - ly fun To
scored a run! and well I ran! Now,

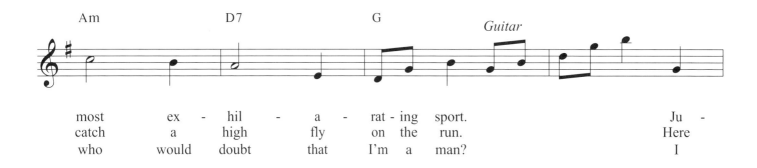

most ex - hil - a - rat - ing sport. Ju -
catch a high fly on the run. Here
who would doubt that I'm a man? I

di - cious peo - ple all sup - port This
is_____ the ball! 'tis sure - ly fun To
scored_____ a run! and well I ran! Now

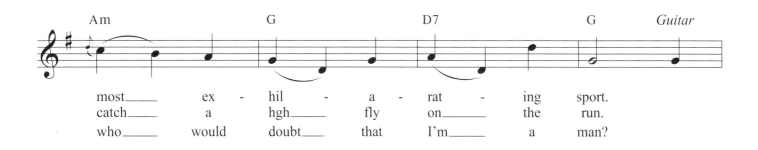

most_____ ex - hil - a - rat - ing sport.
catch_____ a hgh_____ fly on_____ the run.
who_____ would doubt_____ that I'm_____ a man?

D.S. ℅ al Coda after 3rd verse

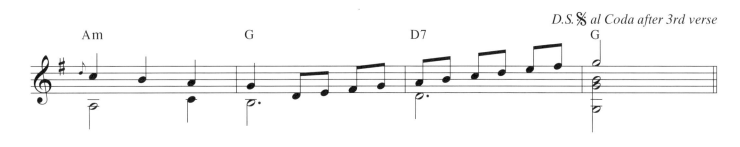

Coda **Allegro**

Ad - mired, ay, en - vied and re - nowned,

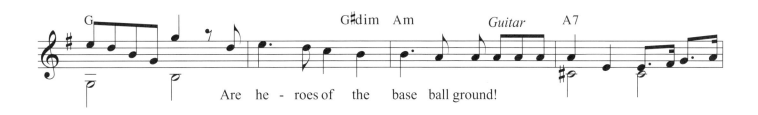

Are he - roes of the base ball ground!

And I? Have I no right to claim That I've just won a

start - ling game? Well, Mis - ter Um - pire, tell me now, To

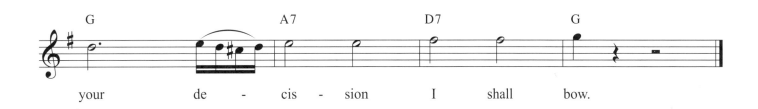

your de - cis - sion I shall bow.

SLIDE, KELLY, SLIDE
1889

Comic Song Written & Composed by J. W. Kelly for Miss Maggie Cline

Maggie Cline ("the Bowery Brunhilde") was famous for her boisterous renditions of those aforementioned pseudo-Irish comic songs. Her signature song was J. W. Kelly's "T'row Him Down, McCloskey."

"T'row him down, McCloskey,"
was to be the battle cry.
"T'row him down McCloskey,"
you can lick him if you try.

And future generations
with wonder and delight
Will read in history's pages
of the great McCloskey fight.

Kelly inserted himself into the song as its hapless "hero." He must have been too busy sliding to notice the misspelling of his own name on the cover of the sheet music—"Kely" instead of "Kelly."

Sliding into second, ca. 1898.

J. W. KELLY'S SONG.

SLIDE KELLY SLIDE.

SUNG BY **MAGGIE CLINE.**

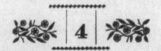

NEW YORK.

Published by Frank Harding.

Musical Million, 39 Wych Street, Strand, London, England.

SLIDE, KELLY, SLIDE

Words and Music by
J. W. Kelly

I play'd a game of base-ball, I be-long to Ca-sey's Nine! The crowd was feel-ing

jol-ly, And the weath-er it was fine. A nob-ler lot of play-ers, I think were nev-er

found, When the om-ni-bus-es land-ed That day up-on the ground. The game was quick-ly

start-ed, They sent me to the bat; I made two strikes, Says Cas-ey, "What are you strik-ing

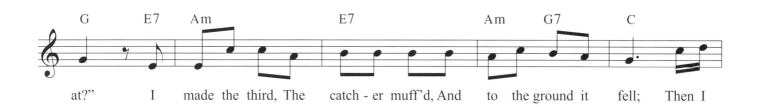

at?" I made the third, The catch-er muff'd, And to the ground it fell; Then I

run like a div-il to first base, When the gang be-gan to yell:

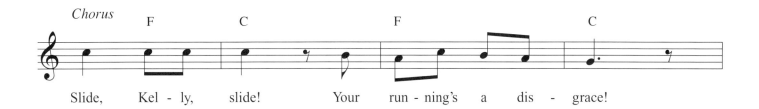

Slide, Kel - ly, slide! Your run - ning's a dis - grace!

Slide, Kel - ly, slide! Stay there and hold your base! If

some - one does - n't steal ya, And your bat - ting does - n't fail ya, They'll

take you to Aus - tra - lia! Slide, Kel - ly, slide!

'Twas in the second inning,
They called me in, I think,
To take the catcher's place,
While he went to get a drink.
But something was the matter,
Sure, I couldn't see the ball;
And the second one that came in
Broke my muzzle, nose and all.
The crowd up in the grandstand,
They yelled with all their might.
I ran towards the Club House,
I thought there was a fight.
'Twas the most unpleasant feeling,
I ever felt before.
I knew they had me rattled,
When the crowd began to roar:
Chorus

They sent me out to centrefield,
I didn't want to go.
The way my nose was swelling up,
I must have been a show!
They said on me depended
Our vict'ry or defeat.
If a blind man was to look at us,
He'd know that we were beat.
"Sixty-four to nothing!"
Was the score when we got done.
And ev'rybody there but me
Said they'd had lots of fun.
The news got home ahead of me,
They heard I was knock'd out.
The neighbors carried me in the house,
And then began to shout:
Chorus

THE UMPIRE IS A MOST UNHAPPY MAN
1905

Joe Howard's compositions include such all-time standards as "I Wonder Who's Kissing Her Now" (1905), "Hello, My Baby" (1899), and "Goodbye, My Lady Love" (1925). He often collaborated with lyricists Frank Adams and Will Hough, as in this anti-umpire blast. As to what inspired Adams and Hough to add the two extra choruses, your guess is as good as mine...

The umpire makes a call, ca. 1910.

HARRY ASKIN
PRESENTS

THE UMPIRE

MUSICAL COMEDY IN 2 ACTS

You Look Awful Good To Father   60

Cross Your Heart   60

I Want A Girl Like You   . . .   60

The Umpire Is A Most Unhappy Man   60

Drums of the Fore and Aft   .   60

The Sun That Shines on Dixie Land   60

Lets Take A Trolley Ride   . .   60

Clorinda Jackson   60

Selection $1.00

Book & Lyrics by
WILL M. HOUGH
AND
FRANK R. ADAMS

Music by
JOS. E. HOWARD

The Record Run
300 Times in
Chicago

PUBLISHED BY
CHAS. K. HARRIS
NEW YORK
CHICAGO
CANADIAN-AMERICAN MUSIC CO. LTD.-TORONTO, CANADA.
ALBERT & SON
LONDON AND SYDNEY

STARMER.

THE UMPIRE IS A MOST UNHAPPY MAN

Words by
Frank Adams and Will Hough

Music by
Joseph E. Howard

An um-pire is a cross be-tween a bull-frog and a
Na-po-le-on and Wash-ing-ton were gen-e-rals of

goat, He has a mouth that's flan-nel lined and brass tubes in his
old, Their light-est word moved reg-i-ments and ar-mies, we are

throat; He needs a cool and lev-el head, that is-n't hard to
told, Where-'er they led, men fol-lowed them, but on-ly came for

hit, So when the fans beat up his frame, They'll have a nice place to
hire. Just think of all that gra-tis come, To fol-low the bold um-

sit. The on-ly job that's worse, is driv-er on a hearse.
pire. He leads them with such vim, be-cause they're chas-ing him.

Chorus

How'd you like to be an um-pire?_____ Work like

his is mere-ly play._____ He don't ev-en have to

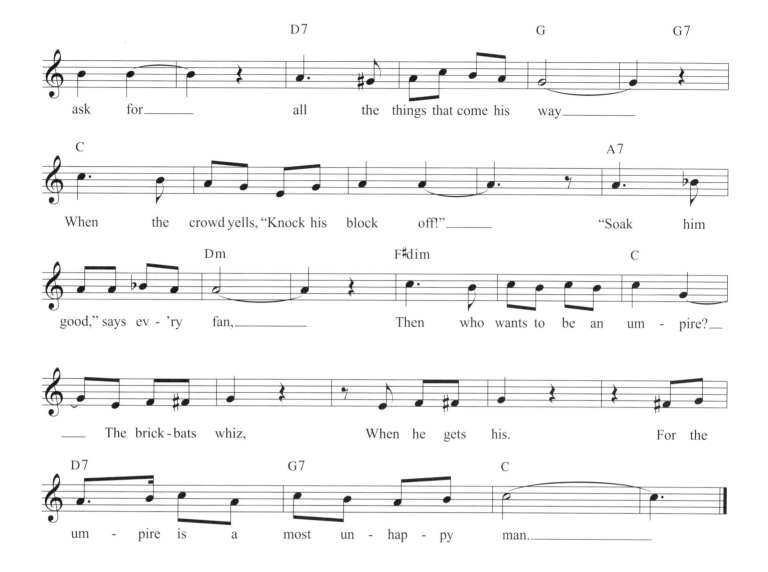

ask for_____ all the things that come his way_____

When the crowd yells, "Knock his block off!"_____ "Soak him

good," says ev - 'ry fan,_____ Then who wants to be an um - pire?__

_____ The brick - bats whiz, When he gets his. For the

um - pire is a most un - hap - py man._____

EXTRA CHORUSES

How'd you like to be a camel?
He don't ever mind the heat.
He has seven lovely stomachs,
They're all full of things to eat.
But he travels without drinking,
Seven days, to say the least.
So who wants to be a camel,
   Without a drink?
   Well, I don't think,
For the camel is a most unhappy beast.

How'd you like to be a mermaid?
Live below the glassy sea.
Why if you swim like she can,
What a cinch this life would be.
But suppose she took a street car —
'Spose the cable broke in two,
Then, who'd want to be a mermaid?
   Gee what a shock.
   She couldn't walk.
Wonder what the dickens would a mermaid do.

IT'S GREAT AT A BASEBALL GAME
1906

German-born composer and lyricist Fred Fischer came to the United States in 1900 at the age of 25. Because of the anti-German hysteria during World War I, he dropped the Germanic "c" from his name and re-emerged as the all-American "Fisher." One of his enduring compositions is "Peg O' My Heart" (1913).

Richard Whiting is one of this country's eminent popular songwriters. Among his best known songs are "Sleepy Time Gal" (1924), "Beyond the Blue Horizon" (1930) [Bing Crosby's theme song], and "On the Good Ship Lollipop" (1934) [made popular by Shirley Temple]. In this song, they anticipate the "menu" in "Take Me Out to the Ball Game" by two years.

A packed stadium, ca. 1905.

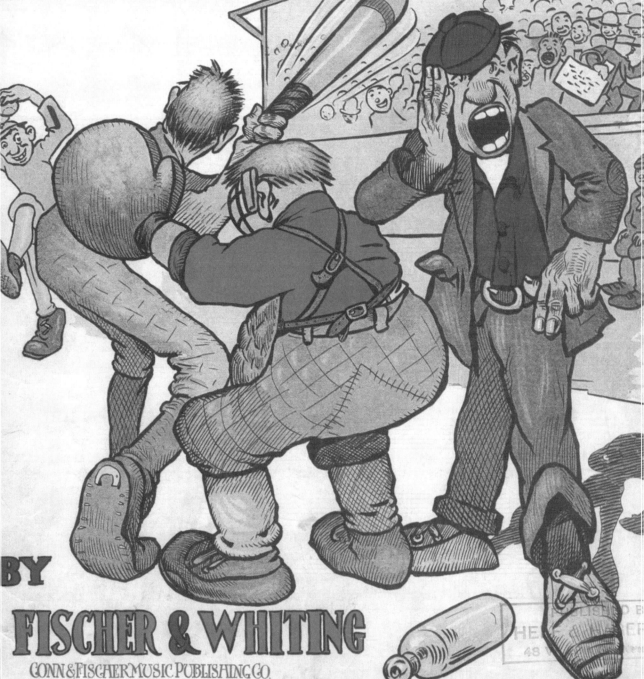

IT'S GREAT AT A BASEBALL GAME

Words and Music by
Fred Fischer and Richard Whiting

Chorus

Come let's all take a trip to the ball game,—— — Don't run short,———— be a sport.———— It's a real Yan - kee game you can gam - ble.———— Don't be late,———— — "Gee," it's great.———— Get your hot but - tered pop - corn and pea - nuts,———— Join the boys in the noise and raise "cain."———— — If once you've been there, you're sure to de - clare, "Gee! it's great at a base - ball game."————

Follow the crowd on a bright sunny day,
Merry and gay, go see them play.
"Bing" goes the bell and the game has begun,
"Crack" goes the bat and that starts off the fun.
Hear them all shout with excitement intense,
There goes the ball over the fence.
No use in talking, it's cert'nly immense,
At a baseball game.
Chorus

BROTHER NOAH GAVE OUT CHECKS FOR RAIN
1907

"Brother Noah" was first written as a poem in 1906 by Arthur Longbrake in the so-called "Negro style" that was current in the minstrel shows of the period. When it was published as a song in 1909 (with what we would now consider an embarrassing cover illustration), the format was somewhat changed. The original four-line "prologue" and "epilogue" had been eliminated.

My sermon today, said Reverend Jones,
Is baseball and whence it came.
Now, if you take the Good Book
*   and you take a good look,*
You will find the first Baseball Game...

...And then the Lord wound up
*   and took good aim,*
And started the very First Baseball Game.
And, now we all know the way
*   that the game was begun,*
And to this very day—
*   It's still Number One!*

"Eve stole first..." was transformed into the chorus and St. Peter replaced Solomon behind the plate. Two other original verses also didn't make the final cut:

Jonah wailed—went down swinging.
Later he popped up again.
A "lion-drive" by ole Nebuchadnezzar
Made Daniel warm-up in the pen.
Delilah was pitching to Samson,
When he brought down the house with a clout,
And the Angels that day made a double-play
That's when Adam and Eve were thrown out.

Ole St. Pete was checking errors,
Also had charge of the gate.
Salome sacrificed Big John the Baptist
Who wound up ahead on the plate.
Satan was pitching that apple,
And looked as though
he might fan 'em all,
But then Joshua let go a mighty blow
And blasted one right at the wall.

1907 World Series, Detroit vs. Chicago.

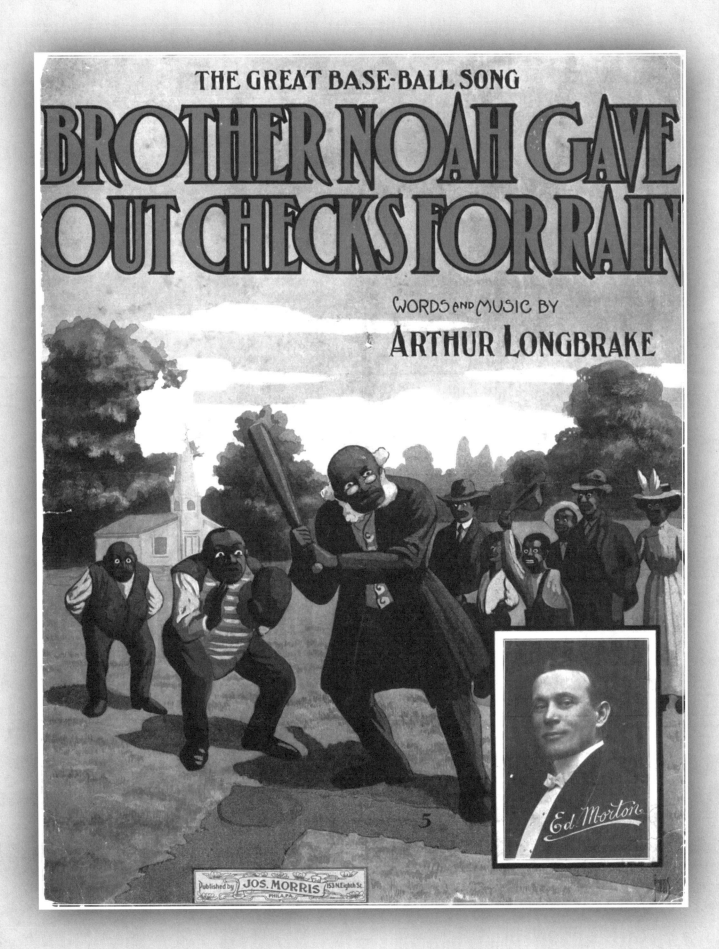

BROTHER NOAH GAVE OUT CHECKS FOR RAIN

Words and Music by
Arthur Longbrake

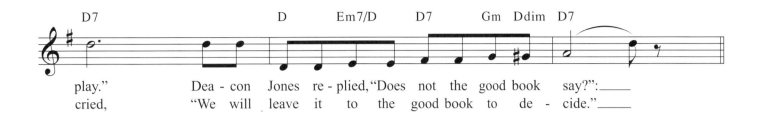

play." Dea - con Jones re - plied, "Does not the good book say?":_____
cried, "We will leave it to the good book to de - cide."_____

Chorus

That Eve stole first and Ad - am sec - ond. St. Pet - er um - pired_ the

game. Re - bec - ca went_ to the well with a pitch-er, And Ruth in the field won

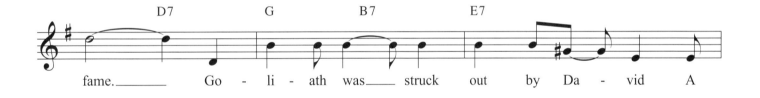

fame._____ Go - li - ath was_ struck out by Da - vid A

base hit made by A - bel on Cain._ The Pro - di - gal Son_ made

a home run, And_ No - ah gave out checks for rain.____

TAKE ME OUT TO THE BALL GAME
1908

Jack Norworth and Albert Von Tilzer struck gold when in 1908 they collaborated on the song that was to become the "theme song" of baseball from the Little League to the Majors. In 1903, Norworth and his wife, the vaudeville singer Nora Bayes, had written the equally enduring hit "Shine On, Harvest Moon" (1903). Albert Von Tilzer was a prolific composer, whose catalogue includes "Put Your Arms Around Me, Honey" (1910), "Roll Along, Prairie Moon" (1935), "I'll Be With You In Apple Blossom Time" (1920) and the unforgettable "Oh, How She Could Yacki, Hacki, Wicki, Wacki, Woo" (1916).

The crowd at the final game between the Cubs and the Giants at the Polo Grounds, 1908.

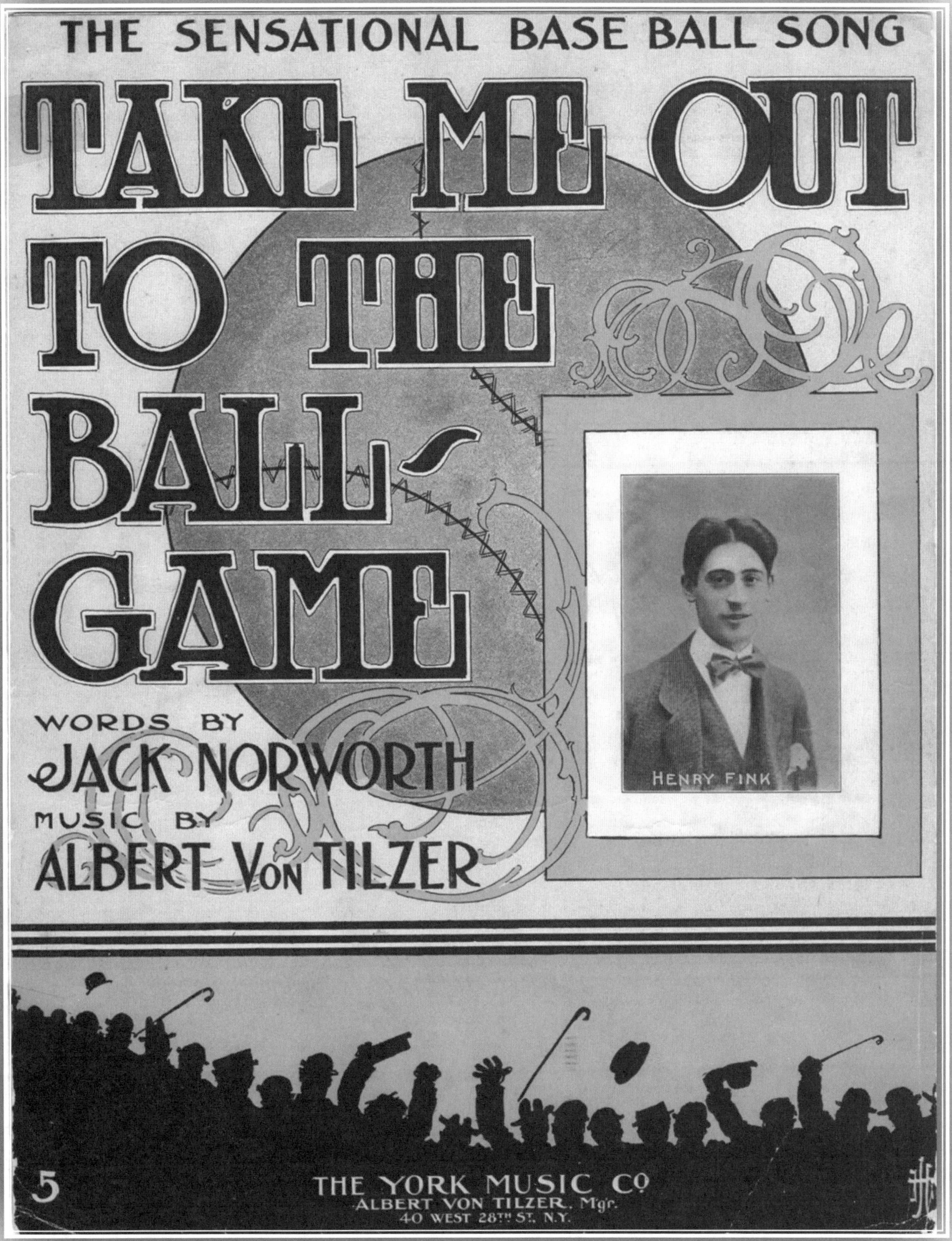

THE SENSATIONAL BASE BALL SONG

TAKE ME OUT TO THE BALL GAME

WORDS BY
JACK NORWORTH

MUSIC BY
ALBERT VON TILZER

HENRY FINK

5

THE YORK MUSIC CO
ALBERT VON TILZER, Mgr.
40 WEST 28TH ST, N.Y.

TAKE ME OUT TO THE BALL GAME

Words by
Jack Norworth

Music by
Albert Von Tilzer

Ka - tie Ca - sey was base - ball mad, Had the fe - ver and
Ka - tie Ca - sey saw all the games, Knew the play - ers by

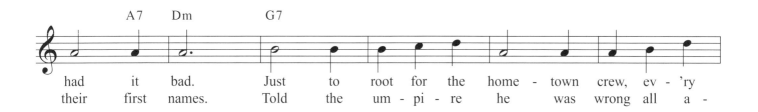

had it bad. Just to root for the home - town crew, ev - 'ry
their first names. Told the um - pi - re he was wrong all a -

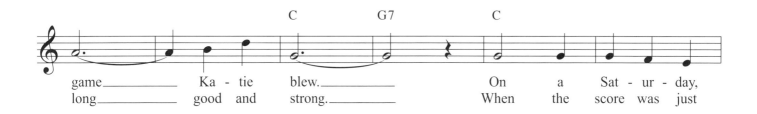

game_____ Ka - tie blew._____ On a Sat - ur - day,
long_____ good and strong._____ When the score was just

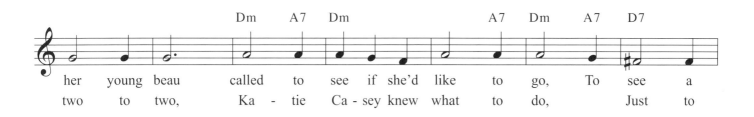

her young beau called to see if she'd like to go, To see a
two to two, Ka - tie Ca - sey knew what to do, Just to

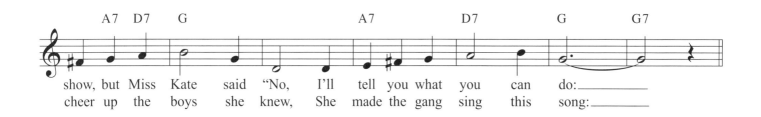

show, but Miss Kate said "No, I'll tell you what you can do:_____
cheer up the boys she knew, She made the gang sing this song:_____

Chorus

Take me out to the ball game, Take me out with the crowd._____ Buy me some pea-nuts and Crack-er Jack; I don't care if I nev-er get back. Let me root, root, root for the home team; If they don't win, it's a shame._____ For it's one, two, three strikes, you're out at the old ball game."_____

ONLY IN AMERICA!

On August 25, 2005 in honor of Jewish Heritage Day, the
Jewish Peoples' Philharmonic Chorus sang "Take Me Out to
the Ball Game" before a Mets game in Shea Stadium...
in Yiddish!

Lomir geyn tsu dem bolshpil,
Ikh hob lib tararam.
Nislekh un vurshtelekh, oykh muzik –
'Svilt zikh keyn mol nisht kumen tsurik.
Un me shrayt, "Hura!" far di shpilers,
Biz zey dergreykhn dem tsil.
Vayl 'siz eyns, tsvey, dray un miz OYS
Ba dem beysbolshpil.
Shpil bol!

TAKE YOUR GIRL TO THE BALL GAME
1908

It is no accident that this song was composed in 1908—the year in which "Take Me Out to the Ball Game" was written. The celebrated composers and lyricists, George M. Cohan ("Give My Regards to Broadway" [1904], "Over There" [1917]) plus the duo of William Jerome and Jean Schwartz ("Hamlet Was a Melancholy Dane" [1903], "Irish Molly O" [1905]), teamed up in a desperate attempt to capitalize on the success of "Take Me Out to the Ballgame"—even utilizing the same waltz meter, phrasing in the opening line and buying "cool lemonade" instead of "peanuts and "cracker jack." It was a valiant try, but it didn't work.

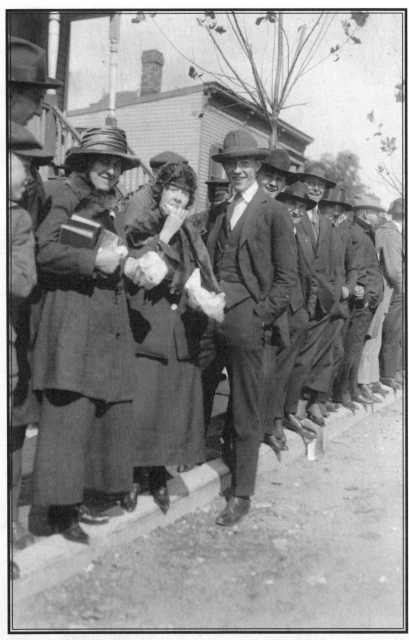

Baseball fans lining up for a game, ca. 1920.

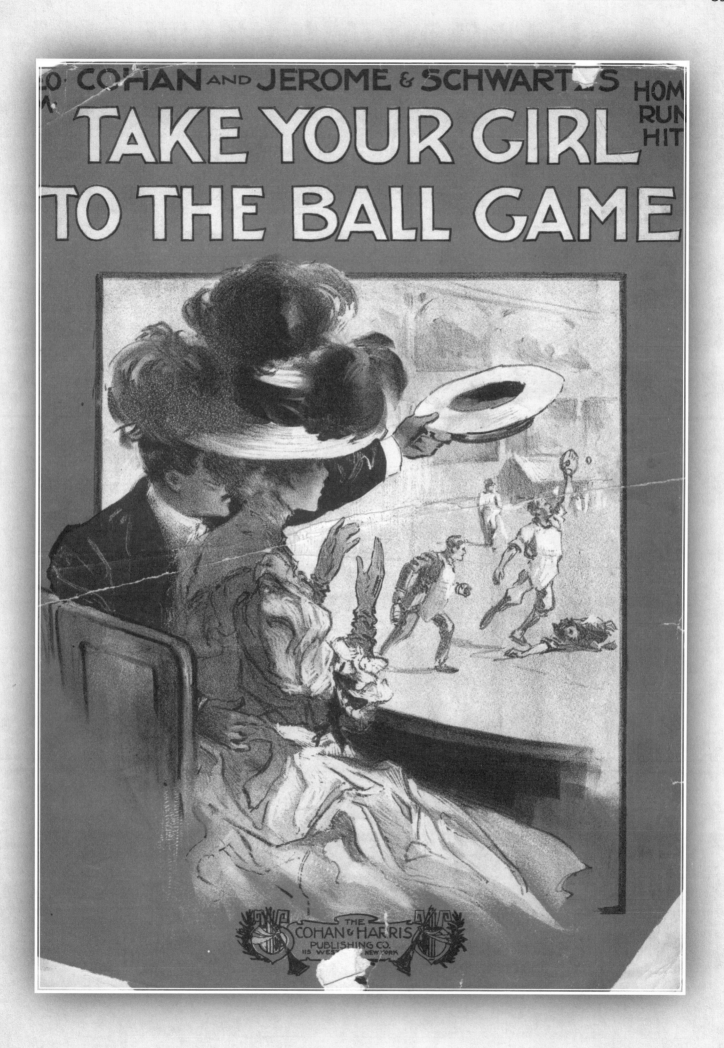

TAKE YOUR GIRL TO THE BALL GAME

Words and Music by
George M. Cohan,
William Jerome and Jean Schwartz

Chorus

Take your girl to the ball game, An - y old af - ter - noon._____ That's the spot to pro - pose to Mame, The spot for a sun - shin - y spoon._____ Make a fan of your stead - y girl, If you lose her I'll take all the blame._____ In the stand it's just grand as she squeez - es your hand, At the Base Ball game._____

Get your seat in the shade,
Buy some cool lemonade,
And a big bag of peanuts or two.
Tell her each player's name,
And all points of the game,
All her life she'll be thankful to you.
Ev'ry real Yankee maid
Loves to see the game played.
For ten innings she'd travel to Rome.
And she'll pray ev'ry day,
That the home leads away,
That they'll win and she'll sing when they're home:
Chorus

When my Mame is my wife,
And we're settled for life
In a home filled with comforts and joys,
It's a family then,
Lots of kids, nine or ten,
And I'd like to have nine of them boys.
Then I'll have my own team,
And can root and can scream.
And the very first day that they play,
As I start for the game,
I am sure that my Mame,
Tho' she's eighty years old, she will say:
Chorus

BASE-BALL
1908
Dedicated to the Base-Ball Fans

Among Roger Lewis's lyrics, which were set to music by various composers, is "Jesse James" (1911), which begins with the lyrics, "Living in Missouri was a bold bad man..." Another interesting song of his, "Oceana Roll" (also 1911), is a ragtime number with music by French-born composer Lucien Denni. The song refers lightheartedly to the American victory in the Spanish-American War (1898). Al Brown, true to the spirit of the times, composed rags ("Rag-Tag Rag" [1910], "A Simple Slow Drag" [1906]), "exotic" numbers ("Yo-San: a Japanese Intermezzo Two Step" [1904]) and patriotic songs during World War I ("There's a Service Flag Flying at Our Home" [1917], "We'll Do Our Share" [1918]). He also wrote another baseball song ("I Want to Go to a Ball Game" [1909]).

Fans in White Sox Park, ca. 1908.

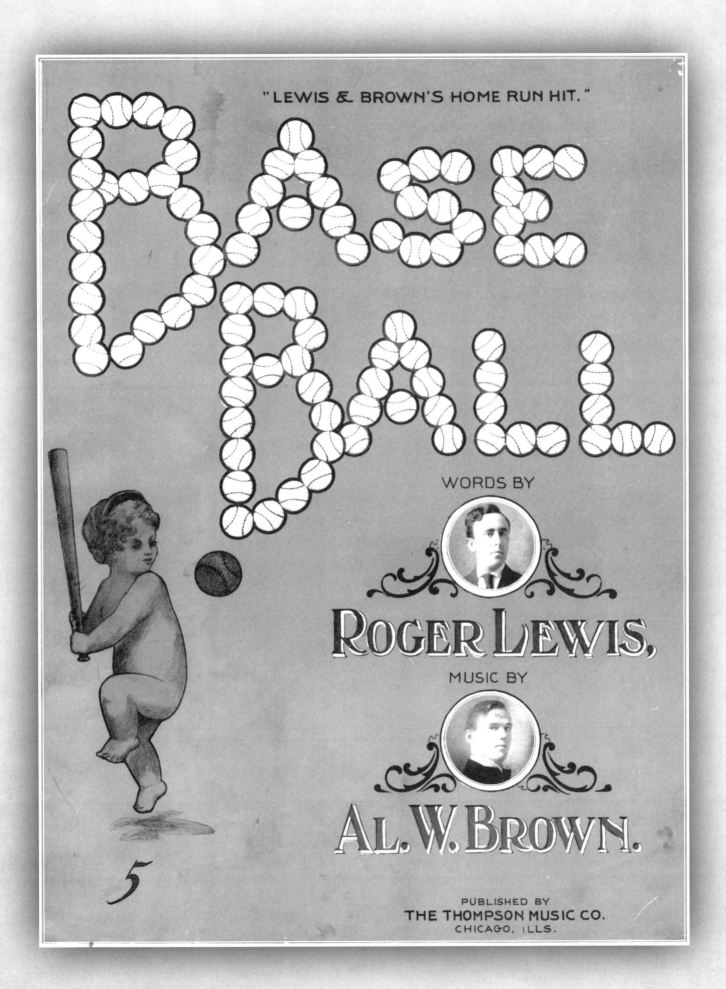

BASE-BALL

Dedicated to the Base-ball Fans

Words by
Roger Lewis

Music by
Al W. Brown

What is the game that ev - 'ry bo - dy raves so much a - bout? Base Ball. Base

Ball. What is the game that all the pa - pers write so much a - bout? Base Ball. Base

Ball. The lit - tle boys will run a - way from school to see the game. Al -

tho' you know it is - n't right, You know they're not to blame. For when you were a lit - tle boy, You

used to do the same, To go to see a game of Base - ball. Rah! Rah!

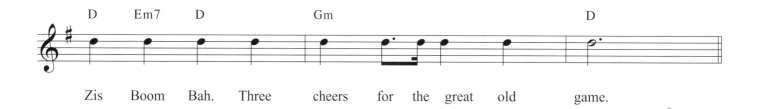

Zis Boom Bah. Three cheers for the great old game.

Why is it little Johnny tells the boss that he is sick?
Base Ball. Base Ball.
And asks if he will let him off to see a doctor quick.
Base Ball. Base Ball.
He's seated in the bleachers and by chance he looks across.
The batter hits the ball a crack, and in the crowd it's lost.
Johnny makes a run for it, and bumps into the boss.
The both of them ran after the Base Ball
Rah! Rah! Zis Boom Bah.
Now Johnny isn't working any more.
Chorus

STARS OF THE NATIONAL GAME
1908

In writing and composing "Stars of the National Game" in 1908, Anne Caldwell and her husband, James O'Dea, populated their song with some of baseball's all-time stars. Here is their line-up:

Mike ("Turkey Mike") Donlin: played in 155 games in the outfield for the N.Y. Giants in 1908. He batted .334, with 198 hits, 106 RBIs and 30 stolen bases. His lifetime batting average over 12 seasons (1899–1914) was .333.

Honus Wagner ("The Flying Dutchman"): played 155 games at shortstop for the Pittsburgh Pirates in 1908. He batted .354, with 201 hits, 109 RBIs and 53 stolen bases. His batting average over 21 seasons (1897–1917) was .327. He was inducted into the Baseball Hall of Fame in 1936.

Napoleon ("Nap") Lajoie: Second baseman and manager of the Cleveland Naps batted a respectable .289 in 1908. In his debut year, 1901, he batted an astronomical .426. In 1906, he batted .355; his average was .324 in 1909. He finished his 21-season career (1896–1916) with a lifetime .338 average. He was inducted into the Baseball Hall of Fame in 1937.

Ty Cobb ("The Georgia Peach"): played 150 games in the outfield for the Detroit Tigers in 1908. He batted .324, with 188 hits, 108 RBIs, and (for him) a modest 39 stolen bases. In 1909, he would steal 76 bases and, in 1915, stole an incredible 96 bases. His batting average over 24 seasons (1905–1928) was .366—the highest ever for a left-handed batter. He was inducted into the Baseball Hall of Fame in 1936.

Hal ("Prince Hal") Chase: played first base for the N.Y. Highlanders in 1908. He played in 106 games and batted a modest .257 with a lifetime average over 15 seasons (1904–1919) of .291. The team finished last in the American League that year. I'm not sure why Anne Caldwell picked Chase in her all-star lineup. There were other players on that lackluster team who might have been better choices, particularly "Wee" Willie Keeler, whose lifetime average (1892–1910) was .341, and who was inducted into the Baseball Hall of Fame in 1939.

Frank Chance ("The Peerless Leader"): first baseman, known to baseball fans as one third of the famed double-play combo of "Tinker to Evers to Chance" of the Chicago Cubs (Joe Tinker, SS; Johnny Evers, 2B.). In 1908, Chance batted .272, and his lifetime average over 17 seasons (1898–1914) was .296. Among his many accomplishments: NL On-Base Percentage Leader (1905), 2-time NL Stolen Bases Leader (1903 and 1906), played with and managed two World Series Champions (Chicago Cubs: 1907 and 1908). He was inducted into the Baseball Hall of Fame in 1946.

Cy Young: all-time great pitcher for the Boston Red Sox. In 1908, his record was 21 wins and 11 losses, but that does not begin to tell the story. Over his 22 season career (1890–1911) his record was 511 and 316. He posted fifteen 20-win and five 30-win seasons. Young was a: 2-time League ERA Leader, 5-time League Wins Leader, 2-time League Winning Percentage Leader, 2-time League Games Pitched Leader, 2-time League Saves Leader, 2-time AL Innings Pitched Leader, 3-time League Complete Games Leader, and 7-time League Shutouts Leader. He was inducted into the Baseball Hall of Fame in 1937.

Fielder Jones: Jones's parents must have sensed something when they named their son. He broke into baseball in 1896 in the outfield of the Brooklyn Bridegrooms, batting .357. In 1908, he batted a disappointing .253. Between 1909 and 1913, Jones didn't play. In 1914, he became the manager of the St. Louis Terriers of the Federal League, batting .333. (He played in only six games, going one for three.) His lifetime average was a respectable .285, and his career ended in 1915 when the Federal League was dissolved.

Cy Young, ca. 1908.

Honus Wagner (left) and Ty Cobb (right), ca. 1908–1925.

Ty Cobb tobacco card, ca. 1912.

STARS OF THE NATIONAL GAME

Words by
James O'Dea

Music by
Anna Caldwell

If I'm some - what hank - y - pank - y O'er a game that's strict - ly Yan - kee,
In the Gi - ants from Man - hat - tan, In the Cubs, as smooth as sat - in,

When I have ex - plained my - self, You'll blame me not at all.
In the Pi - rates, Bos - ton Doves, or Cin - cin - na - ti Reds,

We as bare - foot kids have played it, And the fact should be pa - rad - ed,
In the Brook - lyn bunch of Wil - lies, In the Ti - gers or the Phil - lies,

There is noth - ing in it With our own base - ball. I'm as
There you'll find the lads to turn our sil - ly heads. The A -

dip - py and as daf - fy As a daf - fo - dil in May, When the
mer - i - can or Na - tion - al, Both leagues are all the same, It is

he - roes of the dia - mond Come up - on the field to play.
not the leagues we root for, It's the boys who play the game.

BASE BALL BRAINS
1909

A Musical Novelty by the Bat and the Ball as Overheard on the Diamond

The names tossed off in this "musical novelty" are (John) McGraw, manager of the Giants; (Frank) Chance, first baseman for the Cubs; and Napoleon (Nap) Lajoie, manager of the Indians. The phrase, "On the glad rag glue your lamps" translates into "Keep your eyes on the prize"—that is, the pennant.

"Nap" Lajoie, ca. 1909.

John McGraw and Frank Chance (right), 1911.

BASE BALL BRAINS

Words by
R. D. Heinbockel

Music by
W. D. Paulson

By the play-ers' bench there lay, on a dia-mond one fine day, A

base ball in gown of white;___ Just by her side there sat, her

sweet-heart, Mis-ter Bat, Their eyes beamed with love light. To the

ball then said the bat, "Won't you tell me where I'm at? Why

do you tease me when we play? When I'm stand-ing at the plate, in the

bat-ter's hands I wait, Why do you dodge and run a-way?"

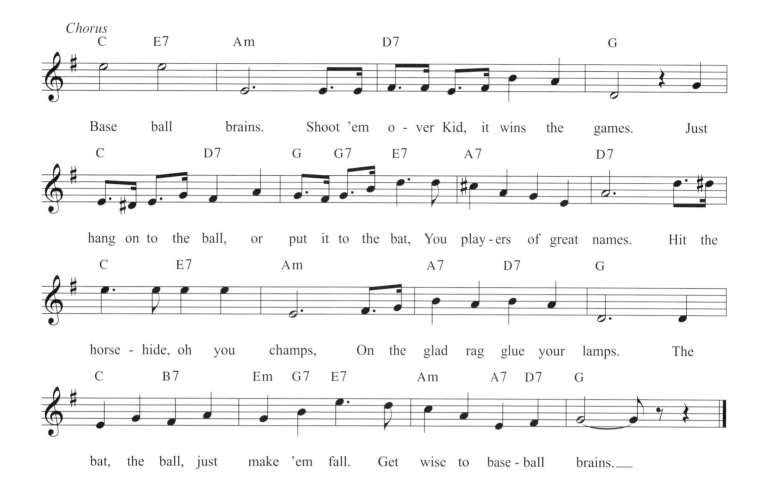

Chorus

Base ball brains. Shoot 'em o - ver Kid, it wins the games. Just hang on to the ball, or put it to the bat, You play - ers of great names. Hit the horse - hide, oh you champs, On the glad rag glue your lamps. The bat, the ball, just make 'em fall. Get wise to base - ball brains.___

Said the base ball to the bat, as he hit a mighty swat,
"I'm sorry to treat you mean;
For tho' you love me true, hob-nobbing much with you,
You know I can't be seen.
What makes me act so shy, when to caress me you do try,
And cause you so much needless pain;
It's the Pitcher, Dear, you see, he is jealous quite of me,
I'll try not pass you by again."
Chorus

It was just the other day, that I heard McGraw say,
"I must keep away from Chance."
So as I passed you by, I wiggled with a sigh,
Near sent you into a trance.
To meet me you tried hard, but you missed me by a yard,
The catcher watched me all the time.
So I could not easily, then renege at all, you see.
Believe me 'twas no fault of mine.
Chorus

Just like a woman will, to the bat, the ball said, "'Bill,'
Tell me who will win the flag this year?
Will the 'Cubs' be in the coin, or the 'Giants' call the turn,
Are the 'Pirates' the team to fear?
Will the 'Tigers' cop the Rag, or the 'Sox' sit up and brag,
Have the 'Naps' or 'Yankees' valid claims?"
The Bat then whispered, "Say? Come around some other day.
The bunch will win that has the brains."
Chorus

HURRAY FOR OUR BASE BALL TEAM
1909

Fred Roegge's choice of the players singled out for mention in this song leaves one a bit perplexed. In order of appearance (and non-appearance), there is no mention of a player named "Larry" on either the 1908 or 1909 Cleveland Indians. "Wagner" is Honus Wagner, all-star shortstop for the Pittsburgh Pirates. Some of his stats are listed in "Stars of the National Game." "Muggsy" is John McGraw, Hall of Fame manager of the New York Giants from 1902–1932. "Lake" is Fred Lake, who joined the Red Sox toward the end of the 1908 season as manager. Their won-loss record under him was 27-17. In 1909, the Sox finished in 3rd place, going 88-61. Lake moved across town in 1910 and managed the Boston Braves, who finished a dismal 53-100. That was his last year as a manager. "Jennings" is Hugh Jennings, a Hall of Fame (1945) shortstop for the Detroit Tigers from 1891–1918. There were two pitchers for the Washington Senators named "Joe": Joe Hovlick, who pitched in three games (0-0), and Joe Ohl, who pitched in four games (0-0). Why either of them merited inclusion here is, as they say in music, *misterioso*. Rube Waddell (Hall of Fame, 1946) pitched for St. Louis from 1897–1914. In 1904, his record was 25-19; it was 27-19 the following year. By 1909, it had dropped to 11-14. "Griffith" is pitcher Clark Griffith, whose record in 1909 was 1-6. When he was with the Cubs from 1893–1900, he had seven 20-win seasons.

Honus Wagner, 1911.

John McGraw and Hugh Jennings tobacco card entitled "Just before the battle," ca. 1911.

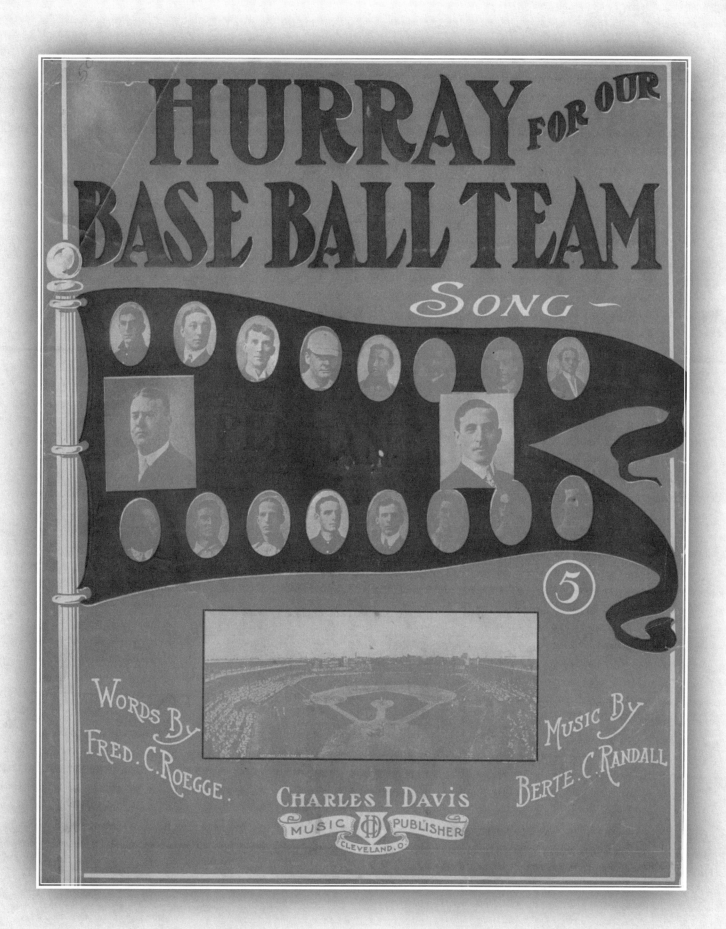

HURRAY FOR OUR BASE BALL TEAM

Words by
Fred C. Roegge

Music by
Berte C. Randall

Where's the crowd all go - ing,_____ Ev - 'ry - one so

glad?_____ Ev - 'ry - bo - dy's hap - py,_____

Can't find one that's sad._____ Street - cars they're all

crowd - ed,_____ Shout - ing [Local town] name._____

Oh! I know just where they'll go, Street-cars signs they tell me so: Di - rect to the

Base Ball game._____ The girls all say_____ We'll win to - day._____

____ Oh, do you think we'll win? Why sure!

Hear the bands all playing,
Fans they yell and cheer.
With that kind of rooting,
We'll bring that pennant here.
Umpire yells now, now, "Play ball!"
Batters all in line.
Then you hear the crowd all shout,
Now old boy go hit it out,
Show that you're a star and shine.
No wonder why the girls all say
That we will win that game today.
Chorus

Cleveland stands by Larry,
Pittsburgh by Wagner.
New York roots for Muggsy,
In Boston Lake brings cheers.
Jennings leads the Tigers,
In Washington, Dear Joe.
There's Brooklyn and there's Phillies too,
Rube Wadell for old St. Loo,
Cincinnatti Griffith's true.
Then comes old Chi, but you and I
Will root for [*local team*], that's no lie.
Chorus

LET'S GET THE UMPIRE'S GOAT
1909

Nora Bayes was the singing partner and wife of composer Jack Norwood during their marriage (1908–1913). She appeared in the Ziegfeld Follies in 1907 and 1908, and numerous other vaudeville and musical theater productions. Bayes recorded George M. Cohan's World War I stirring "Over There" (1917). One of America's first recording stars, her postwar hits included "How Ya Gonna Keep 'Em Down on the Farm (After They've Seen Paree?)" (1918). In "Let's Get the Umpire's Goat," young Jimmy and his pals mercilessly tear into the long-suffering umpire in jolly three-quarter time. (See "Stars of the National Game" for the lowdown on Mike Donlin.)

The umpire is ready to make the call, ca. 1910.

LET'S GET THE UMPIRE'S GOAT

Words and Music by
Nora Bayes and Jack Norworth

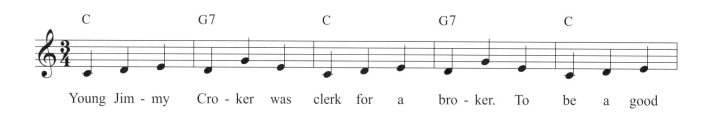

Young Jim - my Cro - ker was clerk for a bro - ker. To be a good

clerk was his aim,_____ When the ball sea - son start - ed, then

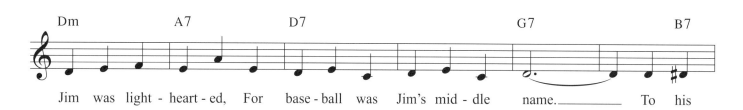

Jim was light - heart - ed, For base - ball was Jim's mid - dle name._____ To his

boss he would say, "My poor Aunt died to - day." So his boss said, "For

heav - en's sake, go!"_____ Then he'd hike to the bleach - ers with six oth - er

screech - ers, And yell if the game was too slow:_____

Chorus

Let's get the Um - pire's goat, goat, goat. Let's make him go up in the air. We'll yell, "Oh, you rob - ber! Go some - where and die. Back to the bush, You've got mud in your eye. Oh, what an aw - ful de - ci - sion! Why don't you put spec - ta - cles on?" Let's hol - ler like sin, and then our side will win, When the Um - pire's nan - ny is gone.

Jimmy kept wishin';
In fact, his ambition
Was nat'ral for one of his age.
He wanted to be
Like Mike Donlin, you see,
And play ball or else go on the stage.
He knew each player's name,
And kept tabs on the game,
And could tell you how pennants are won.
But each bleacherite fan,
Was with Jim to a man,
When his home team just needed a run.
Chorus

BACK TO THE BLEACHERS FOR MINE
1910

In yet another desperate attempt to repeat the success of "Take Me Out to the Ball Game," Albert von Tilzer, hoping that lightning would strike again, teamed up with the prolific lyricist Harry Breen to crank out yet another three-quarter time "I-took-my-girl-to-the-baseball-game" type song. In "Back to the Bleachers for Mine," the rooters are still rooting for the home team. The tune is catchy enough, but, like Mighty Casey, the song struck out.

The original family name of the prolific songwriting brothers Albert and Harry von Tilzer was Gummblinski, which was subsequently shortened to Gumm. The brothers had a niece named Frances Gumm—better known as Judy Garland.

The bleachers at the Polo Grounds, ca. 1911.

BACK TO THE BLEACHERS FOR MINE

Words by
Harry Breen

Music by
Albert Von Tilzer

Chorus

Back, back, back to the bleach ers for mine, for mine. Back, back, back where the root - ers root all the time. I want to sit where the crowd comes in, I want to root for our team to win. So it's, back, back, back to the bleach - ers for mine, mine, mine.

Her sweetheart said, "Girlie, let's get married early,
If you'll be my bride in July,
I'll take you to all games, wherever there's ball games,
But Mamie she just winked her eye.
She blushed and said, "Freddie, whenever you're ready,
I'd even get married in June.
If you will not shake me, but promise to take me,
When we go on our honeymoon."
Chorus

I CAN'T MISS THAT BALL GAME
1910

In 1910, Christy ("Matty") Mathewson, pitching for the New York Giants, had the enviable won-loss record of 37-11. In his 17-year career in the majors (1900–1916), he won 373 games while losing only 188. His lifetime ERA was a spectacular 2.30.

It's a small wonder that Jimmy and his teacher decided to play hooky and headed out to the Polo Grounds for what would be an "immense" ball game. No "peeping through the knothole in the fence" that day for Jimmy. The teacher even bought him a ticket!

Christy Mathewson, ca. 1910.

I CAN'T MISS THAT BALL GAME

Words by
George Moriarty

Music by
Joseph Cooper

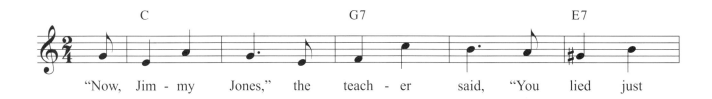

"Now, Jim - my Jones," the teach - er said, "You lied just

yes - ter - day!_____ You told me that your Ma was

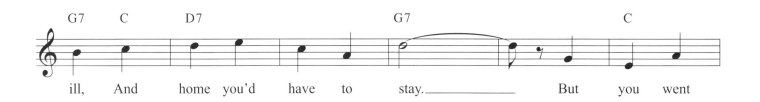

ill, And home you'd have to stay._____ But you went

to the game in - stead, And just be - cause you

lied,_____ Just take your slate and rule, And stay in af - ter

school. Then Jim - my sobbed and cried:_____

Chorus

I can't miss that ball - game. Gee, Whiz it's going to be im -

mense! When the clock strikes three, I ought to be

Look - ing thro' the knot - hole in the fence.

If you let me go to - day, I'll nev - er

break an - oth - er rule. You can spank me till I'm lame, For I just can't miss that

game, So please don't keep me af - ter school.

"Who's going to pitch?" the teacher said.
"It's Matty!"* Jimmy cried.
"And who's the other Baseball team?"
"Chicago," Jimmy sighed.
The teacher looked up at the clock,
Then grabbed his hat and fled.
He reached the game in time,
With Jimmy close behind,
"Two seats," the teacher said.
Chorus

*Christy Mathewson

MY OLD MAN IS BASEBALL MAD
1910

Songwriters, like Edward Clark, delighted in puns and double-meaning phrases linking baseball terminology with the "outside world." Clark really pulled out all the stops with this epic of conjugal confusion and marital madness.

Fans at the Polo Grounds, ca. 1908.

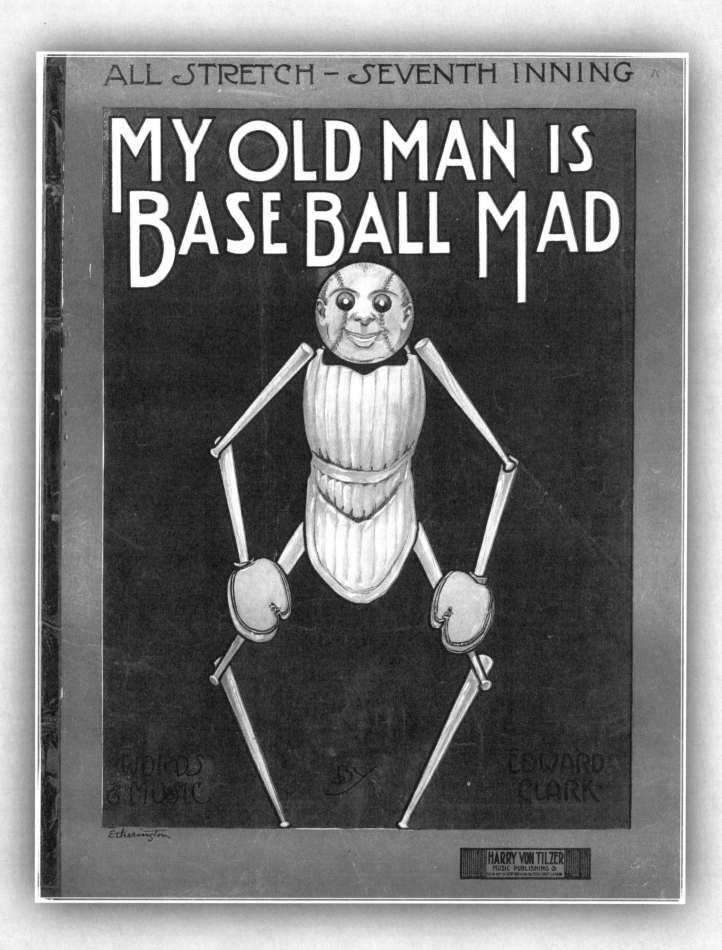

MY OLD MAN IS BASEBALL MAD

Words and Music by
Edward Clark

Chorus slowly

My old man is base-ball mad, You can see it in his face. At night in bed, he

jumps up-on my head, Shout-ing "Safe on sec-ond base." Then he slides to the left and he

slides to the right, And_ just as I'm be-gin-ning to fall a-sleep, He

digs me in the ribs, Cry-ing, "All stretch, sev-enth in-ning."

Imagine this morning, the hour of three,
That old man of mine coming home from a spree.
He aimed at the baby and fired a cup,
Said, "Catch that young lobster, I've got to warm up."
The pitcher was next, which he threw in my face,
Cried, "Hit by the pitcher; Hooray, take your base!"
Then up to the attic he flew like a bird.
Yelled madly, "Don't stop me, I've got to steal third."
Chorus

While even in telling our son how to court,
In language of baseball he has to resort.
He said, "My boy, find out if you she deserves
Get her batting average and study her curves."
Then point out the sacrifice if she agrees.
On a double header then both work the squeeze.
If errorless support she is craving, then say,
Just show her your checks for the next rainy day."
Chorus

THE BASE BALL GLIDE
1911

Andrew B. Sterling and Harry Von Tilzer had a long and fruitful musical collaboration. Some of their joint compositions include "Wait Till the Sun Shines, Nellie" (1905), "A Bird in a Gilded Cage" (1900), and "You Can Tango, You Can Trot Dear, But Be Sure and Hesitate" (1914). (How's that for a title?) To add to the typical "tune-spoon-croon" rhyme of the period, "The Base Ball Glide" included a beauty: "Hezekiah Pruyn." Note also the coy and somewhat suggestive use of quotation marks as Hezekiah makes his moves in the stands.

Some dancing between innings.

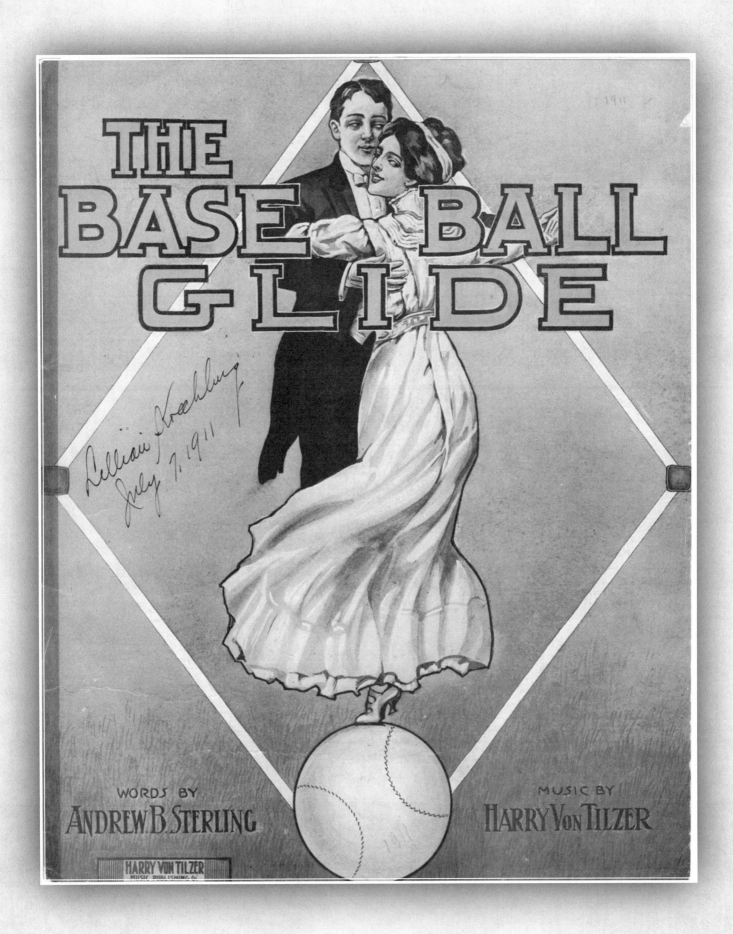

THE BASE BALL GLIDE

Words by
Andrew B. Sterling

Music by
Harry Von Tilzer

Hold me tight, squeeze me like a ball,
'Cause you might let your honey fall.
You're in right, love you best of all.
Wheel me, spiel me, up and down the hall.
Don't that baseball glide set you crazy?
My brain is hazy.
Ain't it a daisy?
It's so fancy.
"Fans" all go looney.
Goodness, just hear them rave.
Gee, I love a band.
Honey, hold my hand,
I can't make my feet behave.
Chorus

GEE! IT'S A WONDERFUL GAME
1911

Ring Lardner had the inspired idea to juxtapose the exploits of "Christy" Columbus with Christy Mathewson, and Napoleon Bonaparte with Napoleon ("Nap") Lajoie. Lardner was a sportswriter in Chicago when he teamed up with Guy Harris ("Doc") White, who wrote the music for this song. White was a pitcher for the White Sox from 1901–1913. In 1906, he won the sixth, and deciding, game of the World Series as the "Hitless Wonders" White Sox (team batting average .230) defeated the highly favored Cubs. In 1907, his won-loss record was 27-13.

"Doc" White, ca. 1910.

GEE! IT'S A WONDERFUL GAME

Words by
Ringgold "Ring" Lardner

Music by
G. Harris "Doc" White

Who lost out in the battle of old Waterloo?
I don't know, I don't know.
They say 'twas Napoleon, maybe it's true.
Maybe so. I don't know.
The pink sheets don't print Mister Bonaparte's face.
No stories about him today.
Cause he never could hold down that old second base,
Like his namesake, Big Naplay', no way.
    Baseball, Baseball, ain't it a dandy old game?
    The Gen'ral of France couldn't lead 'em like Chance,
    So no wonder his Waterloo came.
    If down in his pocket Napoleon had dug,
    Had paid his five francs to see Tyrus Cobb slug,
    He'd have said, "I give up. I'm a bug, I'm a bug."
    Gee! it's a wonderful game.

I'VE BEEN MAKING A GRANDSTAND PLAY FOR YOU

1911

Composer and lyricist Joe McCarthy—not to be confused with the long-time Yankee manager—wrote lyrics for Broadway shows and for Tin Pan Alley from the 1910s through the 1930s, including the Ziegfeld Follies of 1919, 1920, 1923, 1924, 1930 and 1931. Some of his most enduring lyrics include "You Made Me Love You (1913)," "I'm Always Chasing Rainbows (1918)" and "In My Sweet Little Alice Blue Gown (1911)." In "Grandstand Play," McCarthy tossed the lyrical ball to William Farmer who, in turn, threw in every double-meaning baseball term he could think of.

Christy Mathewson taking batting practice with the grandstand behind him, ca. 1911.

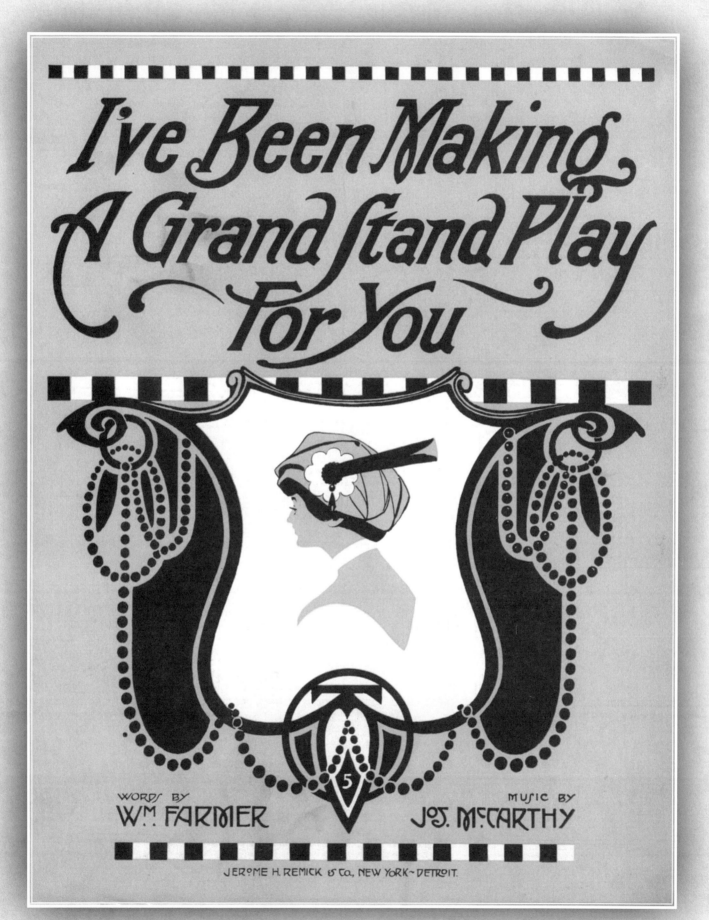

I'VE BEEN MAKING A GRANDSTAND PLAY FOR YOU

Words by
William Farmer

Music by
Joseph McCarthy

Way down front, hand in hand, in the base-ball grand-stand, Is my girl and my-self ev-'ry day. She's a reg-u-lar fan, like a reg-u-lar man, Knows just what to do, what to say. Why, she yells, "Slide, you rum-my," and "Throw it, you dum-my." She raves at base-ball night and day. But when some-one plays grand-stand, she don't un-der-stand, And I just put her wise in this way.

When you threw your first glance you made me take a chance,
And I thought that I had made a hit.
But when I saw your face, I got off of my base,
And then you just said, "Tag, you're it."
Oh, if you only yield and just play on my field,
I'd win the game, dear, for you.
And I'd sign you for life, dear, I'd make you my wife, dear,
I'd give you the diamond too.
Chorus

HOME RUN BILL
1911

While "Home Run Bill" may not be remembered as a major song in the annals of popular music, Canadian-born lyricist Alfred Bryan did compose a number of songs that did attain widespread acclaim. His first hit, written in 1910, was "Come Josephine in My Flying Machine." Another all-time favorite written by Bryan is "Peg O' My Heart" (1913). During World War I, Bryan scandalized many people with his anti-war song "I Didn't Raise My Boy to Be a Soldier (1915)" (music by Al Piantodosi*).

The song included the heartfelt plea:

I didn't raise my boy to be a soldier,
I brought him up to be my pride and joy.
Who dares to place a musket on his shoulder,
To shoot some other mother's pride and joy?

Let nations arbitrate their future troubles,
It's time to lay the sword and gun away.
There'd be no war today.
If mothers would all say:
"I didn't raise my boy to be a soldier."

Frank "Home Run" Baker taking batting practice, 1913.

* Al Piantodosi was the man who started Alfred Publishing, the company that published this book!

HOME RUN BILL

Words by
ALFRED BRYAN

Music by
JEROME SHAY

PUBLISHED BY
CHAS. K. HARRIS
New York — Chicago — Toronto
ALBERT & SON, SYDNEY
B. FELDMAN & CO., LONDON

5

HOME RUN BILL

Words by
Alfred Bryan

Music by
Jerome Shay

thro' the sky. You could see Saint Pet - er cry - ing, You could see the an - gels fly - ing

Home Run Bill, Hit a church and dropped the stee - ple, And the pill

bound - ed back and hit the peo - ple. Hear them call as he swung on the ball.___

Bill, Bill, how we love you, Bill. Hit it for a Home Run, Bill.

One day he hit the ball so hard it broke the fence.
Get the rest, it's immense.
And the ball kept going with such awful force,
That the ball knocked down a horse.
In the air it bounded, hit an aeroplane,
Smashed a cloud, made it rain.
The ball was still a-flying when the sun had set,
And the fielder's running yet.
    For it was Home Run Bill,
    Gee, but he could run the bases.
    Home Run Bill, like a racer at the races.
    Knocked a fly thro' the sky.
    Seven times he ran around them,
    Till the ball came back and found him.
    Home Run Bill, Regal shoes he won a dozen.
    Dunlap hats, won enough for all his cousins.
    Hear them call as he swung on the ball,
    Bill, Bill, how we love you, Bill,
    Hit it for a Home Run, Bill.

Bill was drafted from the minors by McGraw.
Goodbye, Ma. Goodbye, Pa.
All the rubes were sighing, crying when they saw
Him go away so far.
Pinch hit was required to win a game one day.
Put Bill in to make the play.
Three men were on bases and two men were out.
You should hear those fans all shout.
    For it was Home run Bill,
    Gee, he was an awful flivver.
    Just stood there, began to shiver.
    Missed it once, missed it twice.
    When they put the third strike over,
    Bill was sent back to the clover.
    Turned his thoughts to home and mother.
    Home Run Bill jumped one fence and then another.
    Hear them call as he jumped o'er the wall,
    Bill, Bill, 'fore we kill you, Bill,
    Take it on a Home Run, Bill.

THOSE RAGTIME MELODIES
1912

"Those Ragtime Melodies" was introduced in 1912 by Blossom Seeley, a widely popular vaudeville singer, and her husband, New York Giants pitcher Rube Marquard. Rube had a won-loss record of 26-11 that year. They were both going strong. The previous year, she was featured in "The Hen-Pecks," a musical that ran on Broadway for 137 performances. In 1912, Seeley was in another musical production at the Winter Garden—a triple-header:

"A Night With the Pierrots/ Sesostra/ The Whirl of Society." Among the other performers was Al Jolson. (See "That Marquard Glide" for a follow-up on their career.) The term "coony drags" in measure 12 is yet another example of what passed for an acceptable expression in 1912. You may want to substitute "bouncy," "jazzy," "zippy" or some other adjective here when you sing this song.

Rube Marquard, 1912.

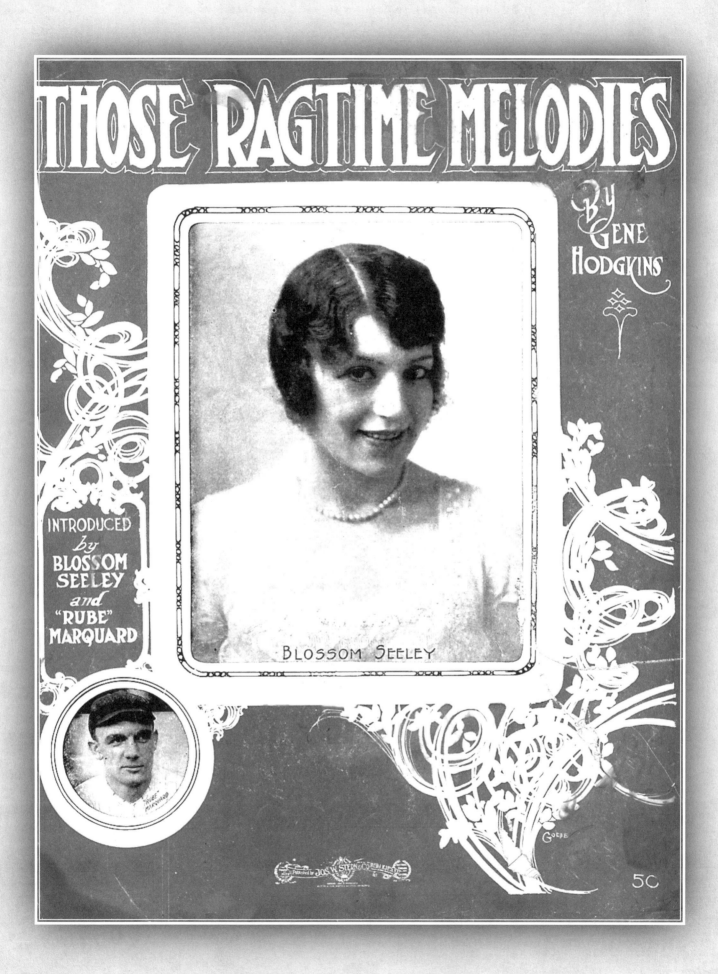

THOSE RAGTIME MELODIES

Words and Music by
Gene Hodgkins

You have heard most of the songs of late,_ Ev - 'ry - one likes some-thing

up to date,_ All the rage,_ up - on the stage, When - ev - er you go_ to a

mu - si - cal show._ Sneak-y, freak-y, coon-y drags,_ Old-time op - 'ra

changed to rags._ Peo-ple sway - ing, Bands a play - ing, Rag-time mel-o - dies.

Chorus

Oh, oh, those rag-time mel-o - dies!_____
(Come on and hear! Come on and hear!)

Oh, oh, those rag-time mel-o - dies!_____
(Ba-by, look-a here, look-a here, look-a here.)

Every place you go you hear a tune,
'Bout a girl, a curl, a honeymoon.
Turtle doves or stars above.
Then some little strain will remain in your brain.
When you lay your sleepy head,
Hum some little tune in bed.
Senses hazy, sets you crazy –
Ragtime melodies.
Chorus

THREE CHEERS! BASE-BALL IS A GRAND OLD GAME
1912

The cover illustration for "Three Cheers" pictures three Philadelphia Athletics pitchers: Jack Coombs (28-12 in 1911, 21-10 in 1912), Cy Morgan (15-7 in 1911, 3-8 in 1912 [whoops!]), and Charles ("Chief") Bender (17-5 in 1911, 18-8 in 1912).

Bender was born on the White Earth Reservation in Crow County, Minnesota (hence "Chief") in 1883 or '84. He was elected to the Baseball Hall of Fame in 1953.

"Chief" Bender, ca. 1913.

THREE CHEERS

BASE-BALL IS A GRAND OLD GAME

Words by
Clarence
Gaskill

Music by
Billy
Parker

Coombs.

Morgan.

Bender.

Emmett J. Welch
MUSIC PUBLISHER
Philadelphia, Pa.

THREE CHEERS! BASE-BALL IS A GRAND OLD GAME

Words by
Clarence Gaskill

Music by
Billy Parker

Fanny had a dream,
Was a funny dream,
Dreamed about the baseball game that day.
Saw the players there,
'Round her ev'rywhere.
Ev'rything just went her way.
Fanny saw the ball when it cleared the wall.
Filled her heart with joy all right.
She could not wait no longer now,
And cried aloud with all her might:
Chorus

THAT BASEBALL RAG

1913

This rag, written in 1900 by Gene Jefferson and Robert S. Roberts, pretty much summed up the all-pervasive influence of ragtime music in the first decades of the 20th century, combining baseball with the syncopation that was sweeping the nation.

I got a ragtime dog and a ragtime cat,
A ragtime piano in my ragtime flat.
Wear ragtime clothes from hat to shoes,
I read a paper called the "Ragtime News."

Got ragtime habits and I talk that way,
I sleep in ragtime and I rag all day.
Got ragtime troubles with
*   my ragtime wife—*
I'm certainly living a ragtime life.

"Chief" Bender pitching in game four of the 1913 World Series.

THAT BASEBALL RAG

Words by
Dave Wolff

Music by
Clarence Jones

curves the pitch - er's twirl - ing.____ Go on Kid, send one out a-whirl-ing.____

Hey! Soak it out, soak it out, Make a home run Ball. Strike. (*Crack*) Safe hit. First base, make

sec - ond, you're____ a bird. (Keep a - go - ing, son - ny, Make me win a lot of mon - ey.)

Don't stop un - til you're touch - ing third. (You're a hol - y ter - ror,

Cen - ter field - er made an er - ror.) Slide, slide, you've made a good be - gin - ning, For you

know that your team al - ways makes a win - ning, When you

play ball and sing that Base___ Ball Rag._____

Oh, what's the use, oh, what's the use
Of a worried frown,
When a game's in town?
A good excuse, a good excuse
Is to be a baseball maniac.
Just tell the boss, just tell the boss
You must see the "Doc"
Sharp at three o'clock,
Beat it to the ball park,
Get in line and holler with the fans.
Chorus

JAKE! JAKE!
THE YIDDISHER BALL-PLAYER
1913

So-called "ethnic humor" was all the rage in vaudeville when Irving Berlin teamed up with lyricist Blanche Merrill to produce this unlikely number in 1913. Merrill was an established lyricist, among whose credits include compositions written for Earl Carrrol's Vanities and a number of Ziegfeld Follies. It is highly unlikely that Berlin knew much, if anything, about baseball. Motivated by the phenomenal popularity of "Take Me Out to the Ball Game," Berlin dashed off this opus, complete with pseudo-Jewish harmonic and melodic modulations. The unfortunate hero of the song (who is insulted with the Yiddish curse, "Poison you should swallow.") is variously identified on the sheet music cover as "The Yiddisha Ball Player" and "The Yiddisher Ball-Player" on the first page of the score. By 1921, Berlin had absorbed enough knowledge about baseball to include in his song "Kitty from Kansas City" the immortal line, "She's so dumb she thinks Babe Ruth is a chorus girl."

Guy Zinn, ca. 1912.

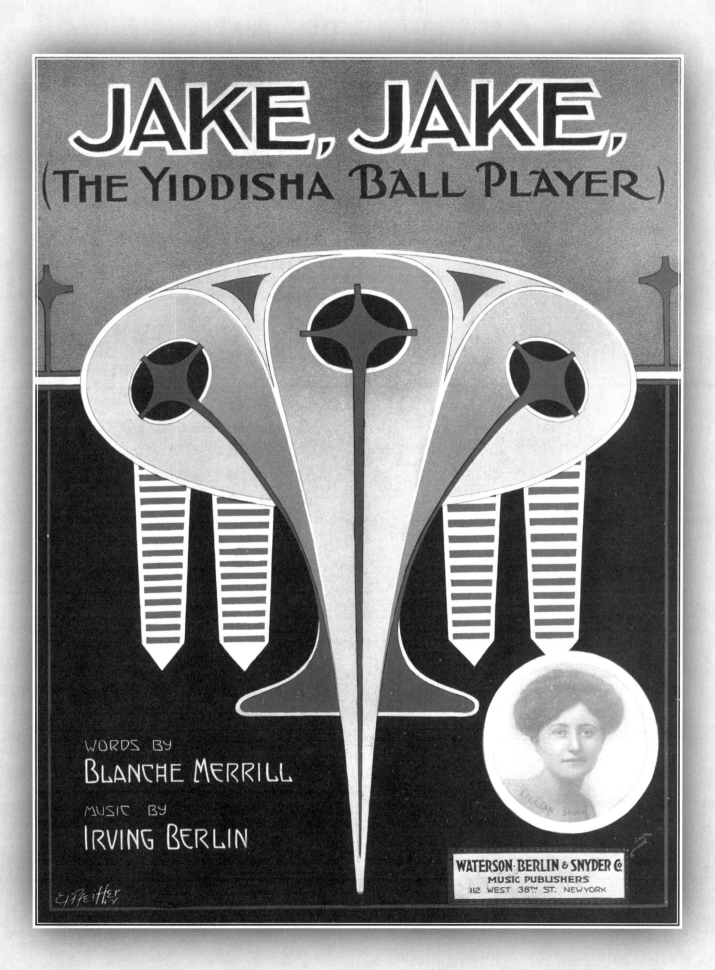

JAKE! JAKE!
THE YIDDISHER BALL-PLAYER

Words by
Blanche Merrill

Music by
Irving Berlin

Hear them howl, It's a foul!
What do you think of that?
Why, he was only fakin',
Now he'll bring home the bacon.
Oy! that boy, he's certainly there with the bat.
It's not over yet, I would like to bet.
Only if you bet with me, you must trust.
Jake, don't stall, hit the ball.
Play with it like a toy.
Make a half a dollar's worth of joy, Oy!
Chorus

BASE BALL [WITH YOU]
1914

Eugene Martin wrote a nice raggy sentimental tune, but his lyrics just didn't make much sense. In the original, the lady in the grandstand is cheering for her idol on the field, but her manner of expressing herself is rather unclear. I have taken the liberty of rewriting those confusing lyrics while retaining some of his general ideas.

Here are the original lyrics of the chorus:

How you take my eye,
How I love to love,
To be your never never good,
But now I'm going to try,
I am going to try.
It's true as I am looking into your little eye.
To never lose to never...

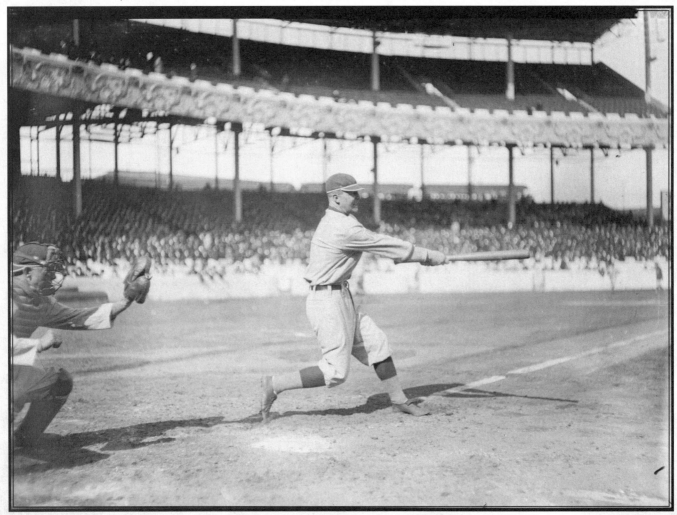

John Henry at bat at the Polo Grounds, 1914.

Base-Ball

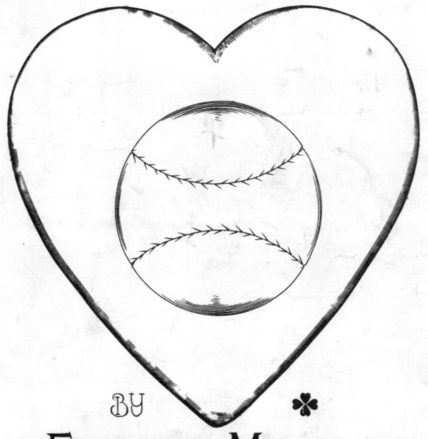

BY

EUGENE MARTIN

PUBLISHED BY

Eugene Martin

647 DAYTON STR. E.   MADISON, WIS.

BASE BALL [WITH YOU]

Words Adapted by
Jerry Silverman

Music by
Eugene Martin

Chorus

How he caught my eye_____ as he caught the fly,_____

_____ And he tipped his cap to the crowd._____ I

knew right then and there,_____ We would

be a pair._____ I'd love to spend

_____ my life just run - ning the bas - es with you,

As we head_____ on home - ward._____ No

great - er game_____ can I play than

base - ball_____ with you._____

When he played the game of love with me he prevailed,
He won my heart where others tried and failed.
It is a thrilling game, in which the winner takes all.
The game of love is like the game of baseball.
And, oh, it's great to be in the lead,
And rounding the bases gaily with great speed.
When the crowd does shout and roar,
I know just what they are shouting for.
Chorus

THE FEDS ARE HERE TO STAY
1914

Whatever became of the Brooklyn Tip Tops, the Baltimore Terrapins, the Buffalo Blues, the Chicago Whales, the Kansas City Packers, the Pittsburgh Rebels, the St. Louis Terriers and the Newark Peppers? These long-forgotten baseball teams constituted the short-lived third major league: the Federal League. Founded in 1914 as a direct competitor to the American and National leagues, the Federal League managed to survive two seasons, folding in 1915 under pressure from the owners of the other two "big" league teams.

The new league sent shockwaves through the ranks of the two established leagues. It affected them financially since competition from the Federal League caused players' salaries to rise and psychologically since star players such as Joe Tinker ("to Evers to Chance"), Mordecai "3-Finger" Brown, Walter "Big Train" Johnson and "Prince" Hal Chase jumped to the Feds.

But despite the relative success of the upstart league and the catchy and optimistic tone of Augusta Gebhardt's rousing march song, "The Fed's [sic] Are Here to Stay," the "two-party" major league machine was just too strong to be long resisted. Baseball fans, who had just lived through the 1915 pennant race, the tightest ever (or since)—in which the Chicago Whales finished in first place by one-thousandth of a percentage point over the St. Louis Terriers and four-thousandths of a point over the third place Pittsburgh Rebels—were dismayed when representatives of the three leagues negotiated the dissolution of the Federal League.

Although the Federal League owners were compensated, most of the players (with some notable exceptions) suddenly found themselves to be ex-baseball players. One legacy of the birth and demise of the league was the Supreme Court decision on the anti-trust suit brought by the Baltimore Terrapins franchise against the major leagues: Baseball was adjudged to be a game and not interstate commerce, and was, therefore, exempt from anti-trust legislation.

The Brooklyn ball club of the Federal League, ca. 1914.

Dedicated to Chas. Weeghman, President
Chicago Federal League Ball Park.

THE FED'S ARE HERE TO STAY

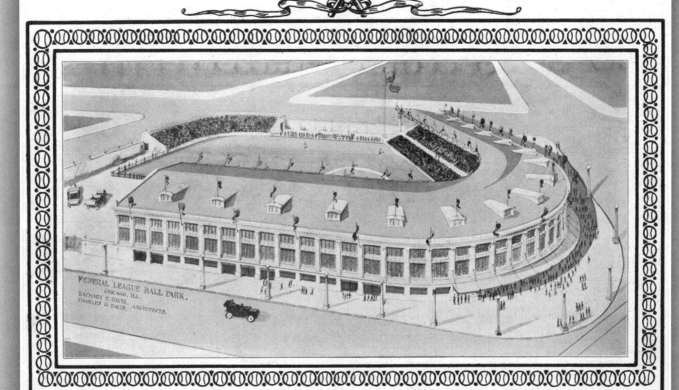

Words and Music by

Augusta C. Gebhardt

—— 5 ——

Published by
AUGUSTA C. GEBHARDT
3746 ROKEBY ST.
CHICAGO, ILL.

THE FEDS ARE HERE TO STAY

Words and Music by
Augusta C. Gebhart

Allegro Moderato

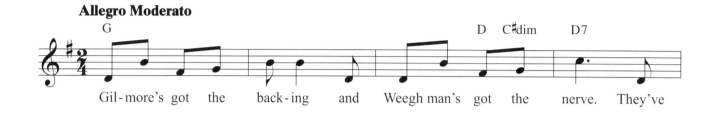

Gil-more's got the back-ing and Weegh man's got the nerve. They've

gath - ered in a bunch of vets, with oth - ers in re - serve.

Come and see them hit the pill, Bring out sis and un - cle Bill, You

won't need an - y rain - check, There's no wa - ter here to spill.

Chorus

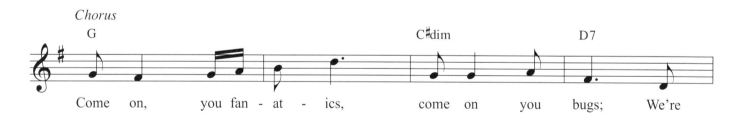

Come on, you fan - at - ics, come on you bugs; We're

play - ing class - y base - ball, like the White Sox or the Cubs. The

Gi - ants have noth - ing on this bunch in an - y mor - tal way. We'll

put it on the old time clubs; The Feds are here to stay.

We're going to win the Pennant, we will clean the other clubs,
We'll make 'em look like rummys and all other kinds of dubs;
We've got some famous players who know how to take the gaff,
Every one is a shining star on Joey Tinker's staff.
Chorus

Then come out to the Grand Big Yard, come out and see them slug it hard,
Come and see them run the bags, they're springing some new base-ball gags.
The Umps will put new rules in play, not like the stuff of O'Day.[1]
You'll get your money's worth and say, the Feds are here and here to stay.
Chorus

The Cubs are going badly, you will hear the Fans all say;
The Sox are not much better, just keep even on the play;
The Feds are coming very strong, 'cause Joe Tinker's there to push along.
Come over to the Fed's ground if you'd pass a pleasant day.
Chorus

We're very sorry for the Cubs, since Murphy[2] went astray,
The old wood shed is falling down, the bleachers in decay;
The Fans will all flock to the Tops, they'll pack the stand each day;
The Feds have got them on the run, you bet they're here to stay.
Chorus

1. Hank O'Day managed the Cincinnati Reds in 1912
   and the Chicago Cubs in 1914.

2. Danny Murphy jumped from the Philadelphia Athletics
   to the Brooklyn Tip Tops before the 1914 season.
   What the reference to the Cubs signifies is unclear.

OH YOU, BABE RUTH
1920

In 1920, when this song was written, Babe Ruth had 54 home runs, 172 hits, 137 RBIs and a batting average of .376. The next year he upped his production to 59 homers, 204 hits, 171 RBIs and an average of .378. If we were to list Ruth's many achievements as a pitcher and batter, there wouldn't be room to include the song. He was inducted into the Baseball Hall of Fame posthumously in 1941. Ruth's teammates mentioned here are Wally Pipp (1B), Roger Peckinpaugh (SS), Bob Meusel (OF) and Frank ("Ping") Bodie (OF).

Among some of Ed Nelson's hits (written in collaboration with other composers and lyricists) are "Peggy O'Neil (1921)," "Daughter of Rosie O'Grady (1918)" and "There'll Be Some Changes Made (1921)," which was popularized in a rousing recording by Fats Waller. And when was the last time you came across the words "cynosure," "foozle," and "forsooth" in a song?

Babe Ruth, ca. 1920.

OH YOU, BABE RUTH

Words by
William V. Hart

Music by
Edward G. Nelson

Now Babe Ruth's a trea - sure be - yond earth - ly mea - sure,

Down in the depths of all hearts, boys. To

reach his po - si - tion is youth's one am - bi - tion, The

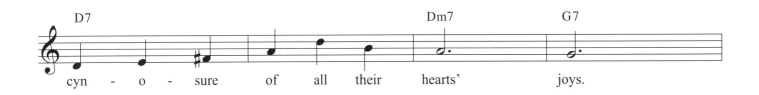

cyn - o - sure of all their hearts' joys.

To swat like Ruth is their dream night and day.

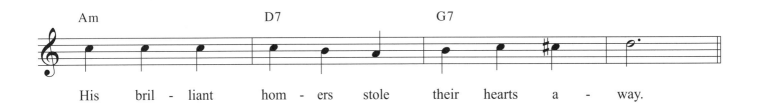

His bril - liant hom - ers stole their hearts a - way.

Ruthism is catching,
It's mighty far fetching,
It has made all Yankee hearts stout.
There's Pipp, Peck and Meusel,
They nevermore foozle,
With Ping they're all there with the wrong clout.
It gave them courage and helped them along.
Here's to the Yankees, let's toast them in song.
Chorus

THAT MARQUARD GLIDE
1922

Continuing the saga of Blossom Seeley and Rube Marquard...The couple divorced in 1920 but were still collaborating in 1922 when they wrote "That Marquard Glide." By then, Seeley's career as a major musical star and recording artist had, well, blossomed, with such standards as "Way Down Yonder in New Orleans" and "Waiting for the Robert E. Lee." Rube's pitching career, on the other hand, was on a downward curve. In 1922, pitching for the Boston Braves, his W-L record was 11-15; in 1923, it was 11-14; in 1924 he pitched in only six games (with a record of 1-2), and in his last season, 1925, his record was 2-8.

This song is identified on the sheet music cover as "The Marquard Glide" and on the first page of the music and lyrics as "That Marquard Glide."

A search in www.baseball-reference.com for the players mentioned in the chorus was not entirely satisfying in terms of names and dates. The only active players found in 1922 were George Murray, a pitcher for the Yankees, whose meager record of 4-2 leaves one to wonder why he was included, and Hy Myers, an outfielder with the Brooklyn Robins. John McGraw was managing the Giants in 1922. Christy ("Matty") Mathewson's last season was 1916. Fred Snodgrass, outfielder for the Boston Braves, also played his last season in 1916. Buck Herzog, utility infielder for the Cubs, and Larry Doyle, second baseman for the Giants, ended their careers in 1920. Josh Devore's last season was 1914; he played the outfield for the World Series winning Boston Braves. "Flitch" does not appear anywhere. However, Art Fletcher, who played 2B and 3B for the Giants from 1909 to 1920 and SS for the Phillies in 1922, could have been called "Fletch"— with "Flitch" probably being a typo in the lyrics.

Rube Marquard with his son Rube Jr.

The MARQUARD GLIDE

LYRICS BY
RUBE MARQUARD and THOS. J. GRAY.
MUSIC BY
BLOSSOM SEELEY and W. RAY WALKER.

As Originally Introduced and Sung at HAMMERSTEIN'S THEATRE by
MISS BLOSSOM SEELEY
IN
Rube Marquard and Blossom Seeley's Skit

"BREAKING THE RECORD,
OR THE 19th STRAIGHT"

JEROME H. REMICK & CO   5   New York   Detroit

THAT MARQUARD GLIDE

Words by
Rube Marquard
and Thomas Gray

Music by
Blossom Seeley
and W. Raymond Walker

Take your place, take your place
On your base, on your base.
Just you hear that band, don't it sound so grand!
Hear them shout,"Hit it out."
It makes a big score,
It makes you want more.
Feel the sway.
Come this way.
Chorus